W9-BMU-922

Love and Honor in the Himalayas

Love and Honor
in the Himalayas

Coming to Know Another Culture

Ernestine McHugh

PENN

University of Pennsylvania Press
Philadelphia

SCHAUMBURG TOWNSHIP DISTRICT LIBRARY
130 SOUTH ROSELLE ROAD
SCHAUMBURG, ILLINOIS 60193

3 1257 01630 4825

915.496
McHUGH, E

DON
015
4/12

Contemporary Ethnography

Series Editors
Dan Rose
Paul Stoller

A complete list of books in the series
is available from the publisher.

Copyright © 2001 University of Pennsylvania Press
All rights reserved
Printed in the United States of America on acid-free paper

10 9 8 7 6 5 4 3 2 1

Published by
University of Pennsylvania Press
Philadelphia, Pennsylvania 19104-4011

Library of Congress Cataloging-in-Publication Data
McHugh, Ernestine Louise, 1952–
Love and honor in the Himalayas : coming to know
another culture / Ernestine McHugh.
p. cm. — (Contemporary ethnography)
Includes bibliographical references and index.
ISBN 0-8122-3586-X (cloth : alk. paper) —
ISBN 0-8122-1759-4 (pbk. : alk. paper)
1. Gurung (Nepalese people) 2. McHugh, Ernestine
Louise, 1952– 3. Ethnology—Field work. I. Title.
II. Series.
DS493.9.G84 M344   2000
306'.095496—dc21   00-062862

for Ursula

Record what goes on in everyday life with as much of your life blood and theirs on the paper as if you were writing about death and birth. In Eliot's phrase, an ultimate simplicity costing not less than everything.

—Gregory Bateson,
letter to the author, 22 February 1974

Contents

Illustrations

All photographs were taken by the author.

The People

In Tebas Village

The Headman's Family

Jimwal/Apa—the headman of Tebas
Lalita/Ama—Jimwal's wife, married into Tebas from Torr
Thagu—Jimwal's eldest son, away in India with the army
Tson—Thagu's wife
Ratna—Tson's baby
Maila—Jimwal's second son
Saila—Jimwal's third son
Agai—Jimwal's eldest daughter, married into another village
Maili—Jimwal's second daughter, also married
Seyli—Jimwal's third daughter
Kanchi—Jimwal's fourth daughter
Bunti—Jimwal's foster daughter

Badhay—Jimwal's elder brother
Atay—Badhay's wife
Lakshman—Badhay's eldest son, away in the army
Saras—Lakshman's wife
Ram—Badhay's second son
Radha—Ram's wife
Gopal—Badhay's youngest son

Neighbors/Friends

Leela—the young wife of a soldier away in Hong Kong
Rita and Mina—two young sisters
Amre and Ammaili—Lalita's friends
Mallum, Bhayo, and Muna—old women, each living alone

In Dusam

Amrit Kumari—a middle-aged woman who runs the general store
Tika Prasad—Amrit Kumari's husband

In Cliff Shelter

Bhimsen—an former army officer who runs an inn with his wife
    and children
Manju—Bhimsen's daughter

In Torr

Pajon—Jimwal's sister, married into Torr from Tebas, now widowed
Siva—Pajon's son
Anna—Badhay's daughter, married into Torr, now widowed; lives
    next door to Pajon

Neem Bahadur—Lalita's brother, who lives with their mother and
    his wife and children

Religious Personae

Maila lama—a learned and respected Buddhist lama from the
    northern regions

Prema lama—a lama trained in the north who lives in Tebas
Tej lama—a village lama whose family traditionally serves Tebas
Dharmamitra—a Theravada Buddhist nun from Pokhara
Tini—another Theravada nun, Dharmamitra's friend, from
  Kathmandu

Preface

The Gurung people live in the foothills of the Annapurna mountains, a range of the Himalayas in Nepal. Their villages, tightly clustered like medieval towns, dot the slopes, surrounded by cascades of terraced fields. I lived in one of those villages for a number of years, and this is the story of what I learned there. I cannot describe the story in a few sentences, nor could I convey the sense of it through analysis. It is about a complex world and the people who inhabited it. It is about possibility and place, and what people make of their places and their lives. It is about fragmentation and loss, imagination and affection.

The people with whom I lived sometimes mentioned that though their lives were full of toil and hardship, they were fortunate to live in a place with *ramro hawa-pani*, literally "good wind and water," which in Nepali means a wholesome or pleasant climate. This phrase evokes not just a sense of good weather, but of a landscape that is kind and bountiful and creates propitious conditions for life. Although people in the village spoke of how loss and misfortune were inevitable in existence, a view shared by most Buddhists, what they stressed above all was the importance of living with grace, kindness, and generosity in the midst of suffering, and of cultivating appreciation and equanimity (a good climate, as it were) in one's own being, regardless of circumstances. The climate in the village was largely one of graciousness and good-humor, with the sorrows of life making its joys more poignant and amplifying the value of human connection.

My involvement with the Himalayas began when I was an undergraduate, in a research project that was directed toward understanding the relationship between ritual, social life, and personal experience. I developed this project under the direction of Gregory Bateson, with whom I worked closely from 1972 to 1977. At that time, I knew little about anthropology, but I had mapped out a project relating to culture and the aesthetics of life. To carry out the work for which Gregory was my mentor, I went to Nepal and lived there from July 1973 through April 1975. Most of that time was spent in Tebas village. I returned and wrote a thesis for my bachelor's degree under Gregory's direction. It was a credible intellectual exercise, and that is what it felt like: an exercise, not fully alive, not quite complete. Gregory suggested that at some time it would be good for me to write about these people from a more personal point of view, to bring the reader to them through my experience. I made some attempts, but I was too young and too close to it. My writing faltered.

In 1977, I went to graduate school at the University of California at San Diego. This taught me the conventions of the academy and sharpened my mind, as well as providing an array of anthropological perspectives with which to engage the world. My advisor, Roy D'Andrade, had the perceptiveness and generosity to help me follow my intuitions through to intellectual conclusions, to clarify and ground them. He encouraged me toward a purity and directness of expression that helped me understand my own ideas more deeply and to develop them as fully as possible. He gave me the tools I needed to live the intellectual elegance that Gregory had revealed to me, the understandings I could intimate but not quite reach with him.

I returned to Nepal for the summer in 1978 and I lived there again from 1980 to 1982 for my doctoral research, each time going back to Tebas village to live with the same family. My last trip to the Himalayas before writing this book was in 1987, when I carried out a study on maternal and child health care for the U.S. Agency for International Development. I have went back two summers ago, and look forward to returning again.

After completing my doctorate, I went on to teach, and am now a professor at the University of Rochester's Eastman School of Music, in an interdisciplinary department charged to instruct students about intellectual life and the world. I have published articles on self and personhood, emotion and ritual, as well as on concepts of honor, subjects I care about and find compelling.

This book is a different sort of work, more in the nature of what Gregory suggested so long ago. Though it is not scholarly in its presentation, it is based on over four years of research in the Himalayas, conducted over a fourteen-year period, from 1973 through 1987. While names are disguised by using kin terms or pseudonyms to protect the privacy of those who confided in me, and names of villages and some rivers have been altered to conceal their places of residence, all events and conversations recounted here actually took place. I have written the book for a broad audience because I do not feel that the knowledge of other cultures should be limited to an elite who are trained to know the codes in which academic writing is couched. I believe that scholarship should be offered to a wider public. From what I see in the classroom and in the media, people are hungry to know of other ways of life. I believe passionately that these are knowable, not just as self-justifying illusions or hegemonic appropriations, but as illuminations of what is possible in human existence. The people with whom I lived certainly believed that one could know the Other and made various acerbic commentaries on others both near and far.

I write this with my experience at the center, in terms of my relationships with people there, because I believe knowing others is a process that unfolds within relationship. I hope to hold myself up as a prism so that the reader can see views of Himalayan life through my experience there. You will also come to know me more deeply through them, as I did myself in the writing, but for me that is not the point of this.

I write of the people with whom I lived in the terms in which they cast our relationship, that of family. I was privileged to be included in a household as an adopted daughter throughout the time I lived in Nepal. It is not unusual for Gurungs to incorporate outsiders in a network of kin through adoption or ritual friendship (*mit*, in Nepali), and such relationships are taken seriously and extend outward to structure one's place in the social world. Each time I entered an unfamiliar setting with the family, I was carefully instructed in the proper kin terms with which to address new people. Their use was considered a matter of courtesy and respect. I feel it would be remiss of me to depersonalize meaningful connections with people by dropping the idiom of relationship here, as though I were rejecting the place conferred on me, so I retain the use of kin terms throughout the book. While referring to a Gurung woman as my mother may seem to some naïve or sentimental, adopting a rhetoric of neutrality and distance (no less contrived than the rhetoric of intimacy) in order to fit preconceived notions of appropriate discourse would be false to the reality of their lives and mine.

This book is the translation of a world lived over a particular span of time. In order to bring it to readers I have eliminated some technical details that might have been included in a more scholarly volume. I write Nepali and Gurung names phonetically, without using diacritical marks or the double vowels that sometimes replace them, because I think these would be distracting to non-specialist readers; I also depart from standard transliterations when these would violate colloquial pronunciation. I refer to the local elected authority as "mayor" rather than *pradhan pancha* because this bears a family resemblance sufficient to accurately convey the nature of the office. Similarly I refer to female Theravada Buddhist religious as "nuns," though technically full ordination for women has been lost in that tradition, because they live a vocation that shares the features of the English category "nun." Explaining the political and historical underpinnings of categories that are not central to the narrative would be, I think, boring and would not facilitate a deeper understanding of the subject at hand. For readers interested in learning more about the ethnographic context than is provided in the body of the book, there are brief comments at the end of the volume, along with suggestions for related readings on Nepal.

Love and Honor in the Himalayas

1.
Reaching Tebas

Why did I go there? It is hard to say. I was looking for a home. There had been so many gaps in my life, empty spaces. I wanted to go somewhere where I could start over and be knit together whole.

In the early 1970s, I lived on the campus among the great, dark redwoods at the University of California at Santa Cruz. There at the gate was the big wooden seal proclaiming something like "Let there be Light," as though the chancellor were God. I liked it there, though I felt different from the other kids. My roommate Helen grew up in a rustic planned community outside San Francisco and had gone to school in the East with Caroline Kennedy. She felt no one should be allowed to build a house on less than four acres of land and insisted that her life was not unusual in any way. I had come to campus on a Greyhound bus, having been ejected from the house by my father who felt it was snobbish of me to want to go to a university when the community college was nearby. It was a long trip from southern California, and a gentle, middle-aged African-American man befriended me along the way. He was going to Monterey to work in a shoe repair shop. The bus stopped for the night in Salinas, and he sat next to me on one of the molded plastic chairs joined together in a row, and bought me a movie magazine. His presence kept other men away, though they walked by and stared, and when morning came we boarded the bus again. He got off in Monterey and wished me luck. I was crumpled, rumpled, and tired when I got to Santa Cruz and made my way to campus with my backpack of belongings. Parents were unloading their kids and tucking them into their new college rooms, carrying their luggage and setting up their stereos. I felt terrible.

In time I made friends, and it was through one of them, Kathy, that I learned about Nepal. She had lived there with her parents the year before she came to college. She told me stories of trekking in the hills and being surrounded in villages by women who would examine her clothes and finger her long braid. She talked of the city people she knew, and how their sophistication was so different from ours. I had lived that year in England, on a scholarship as an exchange student. England had been a refuge for me, being part of a kind, harmonious family who lived in an old stone farmhouse in the middle of rolling fields. They had a dog and a cat and several cows, and our evenings had been filled with conversation and laughter. My childhood had been ragged and difficult, and I was happy there. After being out with my friends I would walk home late at night through the country lanes, enjoying the crunch of my footsteps and the shadows of the trees. I liked the idea of going abroad again. I recognized that during the first few months in a new place I saw it from an old perspective, then after a painful period of confusion I understood it in different terms, terms that changed my point of view entirely and made my old life look strange. When I went away again, I knew I would stay for a long time, and I wanted to live with a family, to be wholly involved and without the buffer of solitude. I wanted to melt into an unfamiliar world and be shaped by it, to see life in a new, unknown way. Kathy and I talked. I studied, worked at my job cleaning tables in the dining hall, and spent time with friends. I slept half the summer in a bedroll in a meadow so I could save enough money to return to England to see my family there, and I decided to go live in Nepal.

At that time I loved the theater and wanted to become an actress. At nineteen, for me that meant standing on stage, surrendering one's self, and embodying truth. I felt this required a broad education. One day a friend told me about a seminar he thought I should take. He said it was small, as not many people knew about it, and was taught by a really interesting man named Gregory Bateson. It was called "Aesthetic Process," which seemed right for me, and I went along.

I walked into a room with a long rectangular table and windows overlooking a lawn. Gregory was in his seventies by then, tall and stooped with eyes like a bird of prey and a hooked nose. His clothes were so casual and worn that my friend Melita mistook him for the janitor. The seminar was intimate and conversational in style. In the seminar as in his written work, Gregory made ideas immanent. He presented them with irony and engaged them with passion. I was compelled. I was entranced. I was converted to intellectual life, *his* kind: alive, intimate, humorous, persevering, and hungry to know. His intellectual approach was not about grasping and controlling, a "command" or "mastery" of knowledge, but about relationship and insight. One day he gave us each a Rilke poem and sent us into the forest to find a leaf with the same structure. He believed there was a pattern that connected all life and that with careful sustained attention it could be understood. Gregory and I liked each other, shared certain childhood tragedies and certain sensibilities, and he took me in hand as his student. We met week after week in his office to discuss ways of knowing: poetry, art, science, and I crafted a project to look at how rituals about death might convey understandings about life in the Himalayas.

I spent a year working with Gregory on this and going up to Berkeley to study the Nepali language. A Nepalese psychology professor at Santa Cruz, Bhuwan Lal Joshi, invited me to come home and be with his family on Sundays so that I could practice the language with his children. Each week he came to my place to pick me up and I sat in the backyard with him and his two sons, near a playhouse painted and labelled "Toad Hall," after *Wind in the Willows*. The little boys and I struggled to converse in Nepali, the boys staging frequent revolts and running off to play ball. Bhuwan Lal gave me advice, scolded me (saying projects like mine were generally a bad idea), and treated me with every kindness. His wife made delicious lunches and told me how he had decided to marry her after seeing her walking with college friends on a street in Darjeeling. (She was sweetly and delicately beautiful.) My life developed a rhythm built around Nepal.

By summer, it was time for me to go. After spending a week with a friend in Maine, I went to New York and boarded the plane at JFK. The tunnel into it was dim after the florescent lights of the terminal, gray and dusky. The Kuwait Airlines plane was even dimmer and smaller than the big jet I had crossed the country in. I buckled my seatbelt and looked out at the dark runway, marked by blue lamps. I wondered what I was doing, going so far away alone. There was a stewardess standing in a blue suit in the middle of the narrow aisle. She had black hair and a small round hat. I heard the thump as they closed the door, the click of the lock that secured it. I looked out into the dark again and began to cry. The engines whirred and rumbled and the plane sped down the runway and cut through the night. The buildings below got small and disappeared, and the city became patterns of light as we circled upward.

*   *   *

I live in Rochester, New York now. It is leafy and lush in the summer and in the winter the sky is vast and bare, framed by snowy branches. I have a nine-year-old daughter who looks like a Botticelli madonna in miniature, slim with long hair and very blue eyes. She asks me questions at the dinner table, like "What is infinity?" This began early, when she was three or four and wanted to know about death and God. She likes me to come to her school once a year, wearing my most glamorous sari, and tell the children about Nepal. I bring food and show slides. One boy, duly impressed, touched me last time and said, "This arm was really there?" I am wonder-mother, the exotic and resplendent, who comes with flavors and photos of strange lands.

After my talk there on a warm spring day, we walked to the museum where three Tibetan Buddhist monks were making an intricate design out of colored grains of sand. It was a mandala representing the divine palace of Kalachakra, a deity of time and transformation. The monks held small metal cylinders and stood around a square black table tapping the cylinders so that grains of sand fell out in precise and intricate patterns, recreating in minute perfection the exact features of the mandala. The constant scraping tap was hypnotic, like the hum of insects in a forest. After six weeks of work, the mandala was completed and lay in ornate magnificence on the table. As hundreds of people came to view it for the final time, walking in a long steady line around the table, the monks began to dismantle it, destroying the design and brushing the sand into a clay urn. At the end, the monks invited assistance, and children and adults took turns sweeping the sand into a pile. The security guard pushed an old woman in a wheelchair through the crowd and she, too, brushed the grains toward the center of the table. Then with drums, trumpets, and flags, the urn was carried in procession three miles to the river, where the monks chanted prayers and onlookers pressed near as they poured the sand through a long white tube into the river. Red and yellow flags flapped against the sky. The sun reflected on the river as the colored grains floated, dispersed, then disappeared slowly into the water. The palace of the god of time was gone; time that consumes all, consumed. A while later, the riverbank was empty of people and the river flowed quietly on. One of my daughter's friends slipped on the steps the lamas had come down and scraped her knee.

In fifty years I will be gone too. Now Gregory is dead. He died at the San Francisco Zen Center, where friends and family sat with him and read his favorite passage about God coming down in the whirlwind in the Book of Job. Bhuwan Lal collapsed of a heart attack in his office just before class, and died in the ambulance, leaving his wife and two sons and a small daughter. My friends from Santa Cruz have dispersed across the country. Nepal is there, but it is a long time since I have been. Like most people in middle age, my life is weighted with responsibilities. My time in Nepal did not make me more whole. It made me more complex, and perhaps more fragmented. I am not the same as I would have been had I not gone. It is not the same as it was when I was there.

*   *   *

The plane for Kathmandu left Delhi at four in the morning. It was a small jet labeled Royal Nepal Airlines, with a picture of the abominable snowman on the outside. The air hostess passed out candies. As we flew, the plain below flowed into hills, then mountains. We crossed the Mahabharata range and saw valleys and undulating ridges below. The pilot announced that the Himalayas could be seen from the left side of the plane. I looked down: vast stretches of green, no snowy mountains. How could I not find the Himalayas? People at other windows murmured in appreciation. I searched the ground. Then, resting my eyes, I looked out rather than down, and there they were, white and stately across the sky. The plane turned into a valley ringed by mountains and began the descent into Kathmandu. Terraces took shape along the mountainsides, green with new rice, and the red brick houses of the city came into view.

There were fields around the small airport and a few taxis in front. I had a note from the wife of the Peace Corps director inviting me to stay with them and giving directions to a shop she was starting, where she could be found during the day. Her husband had succeeded Kathy's father in that position and she had responded with kindness to a letter about my trip. The taxi dodged cows in the road and sped past vegetable vendors. As we got nearer the city the road narrowed, houses on either side, some with shops at street level, cloth or brass pots in sight, small terrace gardens on the roof. The taxi stopped in front of a wooden door opening into a courtyard. I stepped inside. An American woman with auburn hair and blue eyes approached me and slipped a bracelet of jasmine onto my wrist. "Welcome," she said. "Please feel free to look around and enjoy our shop." She looked at my luggage and at me again. "Oh!" she said, "you must be Ernestine. I'm Jane Martin. I mistook you for a tourist. You must be very tired. Just a moment and I'll take you home."

Jane and her husband Jim lived in a large house in a neighborhood called Ganeswar, because it was near a temple to the god Ganesh, the elephant-headed son of Siva. Their two daughters, eleven and fourteen, were soon to return to the United States and Jane planned to stay on for six months to see that the shop got established. This was the second venture she had started in Kathmandu, providing capital and going in with a Nepalese partner, then withdrawing after the business was running well and the initial capital had been returned. At forty-three, Jane had never lived independent of husband or parents and was excited that she would be on her own for a time. She had rented a large, airy apartment at the top of an old building in the bazaar. The house she brought me to was Western in style, surrounded by a lawn. Peace Corps volunteers were in and out, and talking with them I learned about the areas in which they lived and began to think about where I might go to study. Some new language teachers were in training and I became the sample student and greatly improved the Nepali I had learned in California. The monsoon rains swept in and water filled the streets, then drained away leaving the air moist and fresh, smelling of damp earth. Plants grew everywhere, hibiscus and bougainvillea that I had known at home, but huge, growing over walls and twining up trees. I walked through the bazaars, getting lost in the narrow streets and crushed by evening crowds, and sometimes coming across a square that enclosed a temple, steps going up to the deity and pagoda roofs supported by struts carved with demons or celestial couples making love under the eaves. I knew I wanted to live away from the city in the hills, but I could not travel until the rains stopped, and in the meantime happily continued my language study and enjoyed Kathmandu. Jane invited me to stay with her in her apartment overlooking the bazaar until it was time for me to go.

Jane was pretty, with a shapely body and a vivacious face. Her apartment was elegant, with low furniture and Nepali textiles and large windows looking out on the fields on one side and the narrow street on the other. A maid, Golma, came each day to cook and clean and often brought her small son. When Jane had parties, I often stayed in the kitchen with Golma, shy among the art dealers, writers, and world travelers who stopped by. Jane was a devout Christian Scientist. She spent the early morning reading religious selections, and talked with me about the ultimate wholeness and goodness of life and her belief that illness was only an illusion. She said she had never been ill and had always cured her children through prayer healings. She talked about this time as one of discovery and growth, saying that she had always been sheltered and now, at last, she was beginning to know her own strength. Once she told me pointedly she was tired of the long train of people, especially young ones, who passed through her house without showing a trace of gratitude. I realized I, too, had taken her hospitality quite for granted, apologized and offered to leave. She cried and asked me to stay, and I cried, and we held each other, and I got in the habit of bringing flowers or other small gifts from time to time. It rained and I studied, and eventually I decided I would go to the area near the Annapurna mountains, where people called Gurungs lived. They were known for their warmth and kindness, and for the elaborate Buddhist funeral rituals they performed.

As the rains began to taper off and the air became crisp and clear, I prepared to leave for the mountains. Jane was giving a party for some friends.

It got late and three women stayed the night on the living room floor. In the morning, Jane stayed in her room, reading, I thought, or sleeping in. Finally at midmorning, after her friend John had come looking for her and said he would come back again in a little while, I went in to wake Jane. The bright morning light was pouring in through the windows, made even brighter by her orange curtains. She was lying half off the bed with her mouth partly open and her face tinged with blue. I called the others and ran out to get the Peace Corps doctor. It was the day of the most important Hindu holiday in Nepal and there was no public transportation anywhere, not even a rickshaw. Desperate, I began to run. A man driving a jeep filled with family members stopped and asked what was wrong, then loaded me in and sped off to the Peace Corps compound. When we returned to Jane's apartment, the doctor pronounced her dead. People came by all day, asking what had happened, but we had little to say that satisfied them. No one ever knew how Jane had died. John wired her husband, who gave instructions to have her cremated in Nepal, saying he preferred to celebrate what her life had been rather than officiate at her death.

I can still remember, twenty-eight years later, what it was like to step into that room and feel, even before I looked at Jane, that I was in the presence of something large and frightening. The room felt still in a way that I had never known stillness. The only other body I had ever seen was that of my own mother, when at fourteen after her sudden death, I was told to walk with my older brother to the front of the funeral home where people were circling what looked to me like a pile of pillows. This was the satin lid of the coffin, and inside was my mother, with a mask-like made-up face. I was shocked and stood there engulfed by a feeling of total emptiness while my brother sobbed. "You must not have loved your mother," another child told me later, "People say you didn't even cry." For weeks at night afterward, I was left alone in our trailer up on the hill while the winter wind and rain drove round and gently rocked it. I did not cry then either, though the world seemed vast and terrifying and filled with pain.

Jane's friends and I all stayed together the first few nights after she died. We took her body to Pasupatinath temple, a place sacred to Siva that draws pilgrims from all over Nepal and India. It is a blessing to die there and there are shelters near the river in which those near death can stay with family members. Outside the gates of the temple complex in stalls and on mats scattered on the ground are vendors selling offerings and the brown *rudrasi* beads sacred to Siva, which one can bring home as remembrance. Inside the complex, the gates of the temple itself are golden and the temple rises high above the river, topped with a shining golden roof. As a non-Hindu, I was not allowed inside, but would sometimes sit on the hill on the opposite bank of the river and look down on the activities in the outer courtyard, listening to the bells and prayers among the hundreds of stone *lingam*, sacred to Siva, that covered the hillside. Near the river there are wisps of smoke and the acrid smell of burning bodies wafts through the air. Flames lick the air and a few close mourners stand by as the fire slowly consumes the corpse. Ashes and the little bits of bone left are offered to the river Bagmati, a branch of the great river system that becomes the Ganges in India, and a deity in her own right, like Mother Ganges who cleanses all. Further from the temple, there are platforms on the river where the bodies of non-Hindus are burned. We brought Jane there covered with a gold cloth, strewing flowers in her path as we went. The clouds hid the nearby hills and a soft rain drizzled down. When she was set on the wood, the cloth was pulled back from her face and Golma, acting as daughter, filled Jane's mouth with clarified butter, the most pure of fuels, and her assistant Prakash, fulfilling the duty of a son, lit it. Golma clung to me and then fainted, and the rest of the fire was lit and burned gently through the afternoon. This was what the end of life looked like, death without make-up. I cried.

In those days Kathmandu was very quiet at night. When Jane died, I had been planning to leave in two or three days to go up to the area below the Annapurna Himals and find a place to live, but now my confidence was shaken and I felt restless and fearful, wondering if I had made a mistake in coming to Nepal. I could not sleep and would wander through the bazaar at night. Streets went out like spokes from neighborhood temples and twisted and crossed each other. There was no clear logic to their winding, as though one were lost in dreams. Brick houses lined the streets, the shops on the ground floor closed and shuttered, the light from an electric bulb showing sometimes in an upper window, wooden gates opening into the inner courtyards pulled shut. Cows lay in shadowy corners. It was the period of about two weeks between the two major holidays of Dasain and Tihar, and walking by temples, I could see the warm light from butter lamps and hear the singing of songs in praise of gods. The sounds floated down dark and otherwise silent alleyways, voices and bells. After exhausting myself, I would go back to Jane's, where her things were being organized and packed up, and sleep fitfully for a while.

A friend suggested I go to India for ten days to study Buddhist meditation in Madras with a teacher called Goenka and hoping that would help calm me, I did. In a large, low white house with a walled garden, I sat for hours watching my breath and letting all the painful images and feelings pass through me. When I told Goenkaji how hard I found it, "Observe it, observe it," he would say, with his round face and concerned eyes, "Awareness and equanimity." I went to look at the sea before I left, then traveled in the third class ladies' compartment, with women and their children on wooden benches, boys in stations pushing cups of good spice tea through the windows in earthenware cups, vistas of villages and fields and women walking with pots on their heads, day after day as the train rolled across the subcontinent toward Nepal. I had arguments with conductors, trying to eject me from the compartment in favor of someone's husband, and was protected by stationmasters, insisting that I not go into towns at night. When I returned, Kathmandu looked familiar and the world seemed provisionally safe. I had found sufficient peace to resume my plans. I finished the necessary arrangements and went out to the mountains.

The starting point for going to the Annapurna area was a town called Pokhara. The Pokhara airport was at that time a small white building and a big green field. When planes were landing, the airport staff sounded loud horns to drive the cows from the field. Passersby stopped and watched as the silver bird circled in from the hills and eased down onto the field. The first planes had arrived there about twenty years before, carrying a cargo of jeeps for government officials. A friend told me that a crowd of people had come to watch, townspeople and villagers in to enjoy the bazaar. When the airplane's cargo ramp came down and the jeeps rolled out, someone exclaimed, "Look, it's just like a chicken. Its young walk as soon as they're born!" By the time I got there planes came in regularly and not only were there jeeps, but the long street that went winding from the top to the bottom of town was plied by taxis that charged one rupee and stuffed the back seat full of passengers, one for Tiger Bazaar at the top, another for the cinema along the way, two or three more for the airport at the bottom of the route.

To go to the hills, you walked from Tiger Bazaar past the missionary hospital and then crossed the foamy White Gandaki river. They tell me there is a road into the mountains now, traveled by buses, but I have not seen it. When I first went, I walked along out of town, pleased to be heading toward the rising hills. The initial part of the walk is easy, through the low-lying villages lush with tropical greenery. After two or three hours, these open out into a large valley flanked by ridges that start low and reach higher as you go north. Since I went in the fall, the rice that grows in the valley had been cut and there was a clear, dry path that led to the foot of the nearest ridge. In warm weather, the jungle covering the mountainside is filled with cicadas, so that when you cross the valley toward it, you hear their humming like a distant sawmill and as you go up the path through the jungle the sound throbs in your ears. At the top of the ridge there was a village called Nine Hills, with several inns where travelers could stay. This path was the old salt-trading route from Tibet to India. Mule caravans continued the trade, the animals draped with woolen saddles woven with dark reds, deep blues, and golden tones, wearing great tufted headdresses like grenadiers' hats, the tufts spangled with mirrors so that they could be seen from far away, bells around their necks clanging their arrival. The headdresses and bells alerted travelers on a narrow path that they should move aside when space allowed, lest they be pushed off a ledge by eight loaded mules.

Mule drivers, people traveling from village to town or village to village, and by the time I had arrived, trekking tourists, all walked these paths and stayed at the inns at night. The inns offered wooden cots with cotton mattresses, lined up in one big room, and meals of rice and lentils served by the light of a kerosene lamp. While I sometimes stayed at Nine Hills, I liked to go on another two or three hours when I could to a smaller village called Fort of the Moon. It was at the furthest, highest edge of the ridge, jutting out over the confluence of two rivers that wound like silver ribbons below. Looking east, one faced directly into the Annapurna Himals, their shapes curved gently against the sky. Annapurna, goddess of abundance, whose rounded peaks were punctuated by the sharp points of Machapuchare, the Fishtail, said to be the home of the great god Siva. The Himalayas looked sometimes as ethereal as clouds, at other times hard and solid, almost harsh, and at yet others smooth and luminous, incandescent. From Fort of the Moon they were large and present, and turning away from them, looking west, one could see the hills tumble down, smaller and smaller, cut by the river that caught the last evening light, dissolving into shadows and mist as their shapes trailed into India while night fell. Fort of the Moon felt like the still point of the universe.

The morning brought entry into another world. Beyond that village, the mountains were higher, the gentle rolling of the lower ridges replaced by vast sweeps of land, like the cliffs and mountains of a Chinese landscape painting. The paths were rough and rockier. High villages clung to mountainsides and their names defied translation, the sounds conveying no meaning beyond the place. This is Gurung country, and each place has two names, one in Nepali for maps, tourists, and traveling officials, and another in the Gurung language, the intimate name used by the people who live there. The intimacy with the land is lived; drawing water from the streams, tending the food that grows in the terraced fields, walking the paths so often that the rocks themselves become familiar. This is not the sentimental intimacy of romance. It is clear here that nature kills: the flood, the landslide, the fire, the fall from a cliff. It is the intimacy of knowing, of necessity, of surrender because there is no choice. The land is the source of life, and is itself felt to be alive, dangerous and uncanny. As well as being known, it knows, and can confer protection. Women afraid of walking from village to village would tell me that when they crossed the river below Fort of the Moon, they had entered their "own country" and felt that the forces of the region would keep them safe.

I descended from Fort of the Moon to a village on the river called Cliff Shelter, a pretty place with water running on two sides, where rivers from the east and north met. There I had breakfast and then continued up the gorge that went north, walking along the river, crossing it twice on logs when the path switched back as it met a cliff on one side or the other. It was beautiful, waterfalls and ferns here and there, the river bubbling and rushing, swirls of blue, green, and white. As the way along the river rises and trees give way to fields in places, the path to Tebas village turns off from the main route.

The usual path winds up from the river, a snaking line of stone steps that goes up the mountain, twisting against the steepness of it. As you walk, you cannot see the village, only fields on one side, and a sheer drop overlooking the river and a patchwork of terraces, marked by clouds or birds of prey gliding through the gorge below. Along the way, there are two *chautara*, stone platforms sheltered by a tree, welcome resting places on the long uphill climb. After climbing the steps for a couple of hours, prayer flags suspended on long bamboo poles come into view at the edge of the first courtyards. Then tall stone houses appear. They are clumped in lines of two or three, staggered on terraces up the mountain, the homes of brothers in a lineage and their families.

The stone path runs up through the center of the village, with offshoots to the side, sometimes a defined path, sometimes an understood route through people's courtyards. The village is a cluster of white houses with slate roofs, linked by a mosaic of courtyards and paths. In planting season, the summer monsoon, it is empty except for old people and little children. In the winter and most of the rest of the year after breakfast at midmorning and following the late afternoon snack, there are people in the courtyards: women weaving, men making bamboo baskets, children playing, passersby stopping to chat, young women or young men assembling in groups with baskets and small sickles, on their way to chop wood or gather fodder for the animals.

I entered Tebas holding a note from a schoolmaster in Torr, a nearby village. It was late in the day in autumn, and there were some adults and many children about. A Peace Corps friend who taught in Torr had introduced me to the schoolmaster and his mother. The mother had thought hard about the possibilities and decided I would do well to live in Tebas village in her brother's house. The note was addressed to the mother's brother's wife ("Aunt Lalita"), and explained that I wanted to study something and seemed like a decent person.

As a Westerner, I was associated with a world of riches and power. In person, though, I seemed to them thin, oddly dressed, and alone. Older people shook their heads and murmured, "She's barely grown up" (I had just turned twenty-one). A horde of children filled the stone courtyard, stared at me, and felt my clothes. I waited on the porch of Lalita's house while older children went to fetch her. It was evening and clouds floated above the village and in the gorge below. Prayer flags on tall staffs flapped in the wind. Water buffaloes were returning to the village from pasture, swinging their horns as they trudged up the steep path. Lalita arrived. She was slim and erect, wrapped in a blue cotton sari with a short braid down her back. Her nose was aquiline, and the curve of her eyes matched that of her lips. She wore a gold ring and rubber slippers. The children parted when she entered the courtyard. The village schoolmaster followed her. He read my letter aloud and she nodded.

I could understand a little, though the dialect was different than what I had known in Kathmandu. She looked at me. Her eyes were honey-colored, tawny and direct. Her face was lined and wisps of black hair streaked with gray played around it. She drew on her cigarette.

"Have you a mother and a father?" she asked.

"No mother. I have a father." I said.

"Your mother died?" she asked, hanging her head to one side and closing her eyes, tongue out in a mime of death.

"Yes," I said. A young woman with a long heavy braid stood for a moment and looked at me, then entered the house. Lalita drew on her cigarette and passed it to me.

"You stay here," she said. "I'll be your mother." I blinked. I drew on the cigarette and passed it back. It was harsh tobacco, and little bits came off on my tongue. The pack on her lap showed the label; I made out the name Hope in Nepali letters. The cigarettes I had smoked in the capital were called Yak or Rhinoceros—the fancier brands. I looked at her face. It seemed warm, elegant; a smile played on her lips. I nodded, and saluted her, my hands pressed together. She smiled.

"Me mother, you daughter," she said in Nepali, pointing.

"Me daughter, you mother," I repeated.

"With deepest thanks," she said formally.

Thus began my long and eventful association with a Gurung community, a world that is for me through-the-looking-glass, not quite translatable, painfully far away. I try to capture something of it here, hoping as I do so that, as in the Buddhist concept of merit where in giving one accrues yet more, the people with whom I lived are not diminished by their gifts.

2.
Ways of Life Unfolding

There was a wooden arch over the entrance to the courtyard of the big house, opening onto the main path through the village. You could see frames of the world through the gateway, like images on film: a boy with a basket of grass, someone driving a buffalo in from pasture, two little girls running up the path laughing, bangle sellers from down in the valley walking heavily with big baskets of wares. The courtyard was paved with flagstones and overlooked a small garden and three smaller houses on the terrace below. The house to which I had been brought to meet Lalita (to whom I shall refer hereafter as Ama, "mother," since that is what I called her) was tall and imposing, larger than all but one other house in the village. Next to it was small foot-powered rice mill, and next to that two small joined houses, then the other great house of the village, belonging to her husband's elder brother. Theirs was the premier lineage. Ama's husband held the office of headman, as his elder brother, a shy, slow man, had refused it. The elder brother lived in the lineage home. Built at the rounded edge of a terrace, it backed onto the rice mill and overlooked the fields. Ama and her husband lived in the house her father, a wealthy trader, had owned in that village and given her when she married, not as dowry for her husband but as a gift to her of affection. It was more central, built near to the main path, and the porch pillars and latticed windows were carved, flowers, leaves and twisting stems growing out of the wood. The rest of the village rose up behind their terrace, row after row going up the mountain, about sixty houses divided neatly by the stone path that ran down the hill.

I spent the first night in Tebas in a small, high room that overlooked the courtyard. It was a wooden structure jutting out from the small house adjacent to the big family home, reached by several small steps going up to the doorway. I undressed and lay down, listening to the children run up and down the courtyard, bleating and laughing in a game of sheep and goats. I was tired. Ama had sacrificed a chicken in honor of my arrival and cooked a rich dinner of curry and rice. The girl with the long braid was Tson, her daughter-in-law. There were also two young daughters and a teenaged son at home that night. Their house was one big room entered from the porch by double doors, with walls and floor lined with clay, giving the room a warm, golden cast. Three wooden cots were set against the far wall and some mats were spread on the floor near the hearth. The room was lit by the flame from a small brass lamp and by the fire that burned in a square open pit on the floor, where pots sat over the flame on a tripod or simmered next to it in the coals. The ceiling was shiny black from lamp and fire smoke. Tson stirred the pots, and glanced quietly at me. We ate. I fumbled with my food, not used to scooping it up with my hands. This process looked elegant when others did it, deftly popping a scoop of rice and curry into their mouths and reaching smoothly for the next. I was all elbows and wrists, angular and clumsy, not rounded and delicate like them. I felt awkward. Sitting cross-legged, my back hurt and my knees jutted up like a grasshopper's rather than lying neatly on the floor. The little girls peered at me and Seyli, the older one, smiled.

"Eat, eat," Ama said, and Tson spooned more rice onto my plate. "Come," Ama said as she led me across the courtyard after dinner. It was dark, but there was some light from the moon. Ama carried a flashlight and Seyli followed us, watching shyly from the corner as Ama arranged the bedding. A couple of neighbor children hung like barnacles from the sides of the structure, staring through the spaces between the boards until she shouted at them and they ran away. "Sleep now," she said as she turned to go. From the window I could see her cross the courtyard with Seyli, the beam of her flashlight and the red glow of her cigarette. They went up the porch steps and closed the double doors behind them, so that the warm mouth of the house turned dark. I lay there wondering what strange world I had entered, feeling the full force of my helplessness.

* * *

I always liked sleeping in that room. It was high, a little above but near the comings and goings of the household. Unlike the spaces I later inhabited there, with their shuttered windows and clay-lined stone walls, this one allowed the morning light in. Gentle sun filtered through the boards, softly reaching through the open spaces between the slats. It also admitted sound. The rooster's crow and the pre-dawn thump of the the rice mill penetrated everywhere, but in that high room I could hear the rustle of clothes and the padding of footsteps, quiet voices, the rush of bamboo baskets being separated, the soft clump of the copper water jar being taken out to collect water at the stream. The light and sound intermingled and eased me to wakefulness, feeling already a part of the day. But this was later, when I was accustomed to the rhythm of the days there and people were accustomed to me.

* * *

The first morning when I awoke in that room what I saw were several pairs of brown eyes belonging to the village children. In polite Kathmandu Nepali, I said, "Please go." They laughed uproariously. Two or three of them imitated me. I was embarrassed to get up in my nightgown and remained in bed, but sat up. They talked and stared. "Where . . . is . . . your . . . lover?" said one boy in careful and precise English. He said something quickly in Nepali and they all laughed. I sat there, speechless and nonplussed, feeling angry and trapped. Then I heard the sweet sound of Ama's raging voice and they all scattered, allowing the light to come through and me to get out of bed. As I swung my feet to the floor the door opened and Ama entered, followed by Seyli carrying a clear glass tumbler filled with tea. "Seyli really likes you," said Ama. "She asked if she could bring you tea this morning."

Nepali tea is sweet and rich, milky and warm with spices. I make it at home sometimes and serve it to my friends. I boil ginger, cardamon, and sugar for a long time, then fill the pot with milk and add the tea after it boils. In the village, they boiled the tea with the spices all morning, but the richness of the buffalo milk cut the bitterness. When it was just family, sometimes the tea would be made with salt rather than expensive sugar, but when I was new to the household, I was given sweet tea each morning. I wrapped my hand around the ridges of the glass, feeling the warmth of the liquid inside, and enjoyed each mouthful.

Now Ama returned to the house and Seyli stayed, standing against the wall while I sat at the edge of the bed and drank the good tea she had brought. She watched and smiled, and picked up some of the clothes I had draped at the end of the bed and examined them. I took the long skirt and pulled it on under my nightgown and discreetly slipped a blouse over that, not minding her interested presence. Then I brushed my hair and braided it, and we crossed the courtyard together and entered the house for breakfast.

Seyli was eleven when I came to Tebas, slim, strong, and very fair. She was like her mother: the same lilting mouth and curved eyes, soft pale brown, almost yellow, like a lion's. Her hair was the same color as her eyes. "She looks like your sister," Ama said. In the mornings she would take off with her basket and sickle to cut fodder for the animals or wood in the jungle. She was proud and never cried when hurt, scolded, or struck, but people said she was a little wild. She once burned off a hillside napping after having made a fire to heat some lunch and she was a skillful and daring swimmer, who twice jumped into the river to save other children who could not manage the turbulence of the water or the strength of the current. Like Ama, she had a deep sense of honor.

There were other family members. At home were Maila, a teenage son, Seyli, and her four-year old sister, Kanchi. Their father had been away at a district political meeting for a few days when I came but was warm and genial when he arrived, saying he had heard about me from people on the trail, that I had been sent by his sister from Torr. I called him Apa (father). Tson was the wife of the eldest son, a soldier who had recently left for the Indian army, and was then at the beginning of her first pregnancy.

Living apart from the family were two married daughters, in their twenties, and the youngest son, Saila. Agai, the eldest daughter, had a little boy and lived in a village a few hours' walk away. She often came for visits. Maili, the second daughter, was in Hong Kong with her Gurkha husband. Saila, in his early teens, was living with relatives in Torr so that he could continue his education in the high school there. A girl near Maila's age, perhaps sixteen, also lived with the family. Plump and solid, her round face dotted with freckles, she was called Bunti and helped with house and field work. She was from another area, but her mother had gone off with a lover when she was very small, leaving her with a grandmother who lived in Tebas. Several years before I arrived, the grandmother had died and Ama's family had taken her in. She, too, called Lalita "Ama," worked hard when there were tasks, and then went off with her friends, whispering and laughing. When she came home, Seyli often moved to sit close to her.

Seyli and Bunti went off after breakfast with their baskets and some friends. Mats were spread in the courtyard, and Ama and Tson loosed their hair and began to comb it. The morning sun had just begun to creep across the stones, warm and penetrating. The courtyard looked out over the slate roofs of the houses on the terrace below, and beyond to the mountain on the other side of the deep gorge. There was a village there, straight across from Tebas like a mirror image. Terraced fields cascaded below it, as in Tebas, and above was forest. Birds of prey wheeled in the gorge, swooping down then soaring above us, the morning sun filtering through their wings.

Everything was vertical. The path was a series of steps, a staircase going through the village and down the mountain. From each courtyard was a drop-off to the garden or the home below. Courtyards on the same terrace interconnected, so that people going about their tasks would walk past the house on their way to the main path, carrying a water jug en route to the stream, a sickle and basket for collecting fodder, or a stick to drive the buffalo lumbering ahead. As the women of Ama's family sat oiling and braiding their hair in the sun, people on the way to their work greeted them. When the workers had gone off, two or three older women and some teenage girls came to sit in the courtyard. The girls asked after Seyli and Bunti, who had gone to cut wood. Seeing me, they decided to linger a while before going on. One girl took my arm and began to talk rapidly to her friends. The only word I caught was "white."

The women inspected me. I did not know how to wear Nepali clothes at that time, but had tried to cover my body properly, with a skirt that came down to my ankles and a loose blouse. "What are these white-people's clothes?" asked an old woman, motioning me to stand up. She pulled at my skirt and shook her head. "Not good," she said. The others nodded. "This," a young woman displayed her *lungi*, a circle of cloth wrapped around and tucked into a cotton petticoat underneath. She separated the two layers of cloth and showed them to me, then fingered my skirt. "Only that; not good," she said. "Petticoat." I got the idea that I seemed to have been walking around in an undergarment. I looked at my skirt and said, "Not good." They smiled. A flood of Nepali followed. I caught a few words.

Another old woman, bent and dressed in rags, approached us. She looked into my face and spoke to me. "She can't talk," Ama said. I felt a little hurt. The same young woman who had showed me her lungi took my hand. She pulled back my sleeve and touched the skin. "Are you a widow?" she asked. I did not understand. "Dead husband?" she asked. The others laughed. "No marriage," I replied. She showed me her wrist, decorated with red glass bangles. They looked pretty in the sun and jingled when she moved. "Wear these," she said. "Only widows keep bare arms. When your husband dies, they break your bangles and you never wear them any-more." She made a chopping motion with her arm to show how this was done. I imagined round, red shards of glass lying on the stone, markers of a shattered life. I also got her point: I needed bangles.

Within a few days, I went down to the general store at Dusam, by the river. By the look of it, the general store was all there was to Dusam, but actually there were two or three other houses scattered among the rice fields. The store was run by Amrit Kumari and her husband, Tika Prasad. It faced onto the main trail and Tika Prasad had three or four mules that he used to bring goods in and out. The store consisted of a large open room facing a stone porch that overlooked the trail. Bolts of cloth lined one wall, and on another were boxes of batteries and matches, some canned goods for tourists, large bottles of Star beer (made in Nepal), some combs, rib-bons, a big canister of kerosene, a few rubber slippers. Hanging above the cloth was a large mirror in which, reflected with friends, I could see how pale and strange looking I was, with my round eyes and reddish-brown hair, an impression that increased the longer I stayed. At that time I still looked pretty normal to myself and everyone else seemed dark and exotic. There were mats on the floor of the store and a bench along the side wall. On the other side of the porch was a kitchen where Amrit Kumari sold cups of tea, liquor, and sometimes snacks. She was a sturdy middle-aged woman with a dark pock-marked face, very forthright and often sardonic. She sprinkled her speech with exclamations like "Eat a cow!" (not done in Nepal) and "Your mother's vagina!" to add emphasis and assure hearers of her truthfulness, being a woman of great confidence and strong opinions, most of them negative. She transformed my name to *unais-din*, "nineteen days," and told me that while fair skin was all very well, being, like white-people, pale to the point of bloodlessness was too much. We all looked like corpses, she said. At the same time, she always invited me to sit with her in the shop, offered tea, and usually threw in a little something for free.

A trip to the shop was a festive occasion. It was an hour or so down the mountain from the village and about two hours back up again. I usually went with Ama or with friends, young daughters-in-law of our lineage households who were happy to have some time away from their chores. When Amrit Kumari was busy in the kitchen we curled up in the shop together and napped on the mats, waiting for her to attend to us. The trail unfurled below her porch and we watched travelers pass by, calling out to those we knew. Sometimes I would be called upon to interview tourists.

"Ask them where they're from."

"They're from Sweden."

"Are they married?"

"Er, my friends would like to know if you are married. No, they're not married."

"Ask them if they stay together."

"I'm not sure that would be polite."

"Ask them."

"Yes, they stay together."

"Isn't she afraid?"

"I think they have to go now."

One day a well-dressed Tibetan man and woman rode past on two beautiful horses. "Do you know who that was?" asked Tika Prasad.

"No," I answered.

"It was the King of Mustang and his wife."

"Oh," I replied, astonished, as the rump of her gray horse continued down the path. Mustang was a Tibetan region several days north, on a great plateau, wild and windswept.

Yes," said a woman sitting nearby. "He has no heir, but he loves his wife so much that he has never taken a second one, though he has the right."

"Oh," I said, looking at his erect back rising from the saddle, the hair wound round his head in the traditional braid. We watched until they disappeared around the bend.

The first few weeks I lived there, though, my conversations were limited exchanges. I sat out on the courtyard with my language books and studied, and people would stop for a diversion and chat with me. Though their dialect of Nepali was simpler in some ways than the more formal language of the city it was different from what I was used to. Life was complicated by the fact that people also spoke the Gurung language, which was more closely related to Tibetan and Chinese than to European languages. It was the mother tongue, though people were fluent in Nepali by middle childhood. "It's easy," said my friends of Gurung, "Even the smallest children speak it." The languages were like two streams flowing side by side and sometimes crossing, as people would switch in the middle of a conversation from one to the other, so that a story I was following would suddenly grow opaque, like a stream flowing underground into the dark, and then return again, left, for me, with a large gap in the middle. I came to love Gurung, though I never spoke it well. It was the language of the hearth, of blood and kin, that with its fine gradations of relationship, of belonging, marked one as *rhonse mai*, "our own person." It was a language of mountains.

In Gurung, you cannot simply arrive. You must come from above or below. The general question asked in the village is "Ki kanner ali kala?" which means "From where did you come (below)?" The village being high on the mountainside with only the forest directly above it, and the whole great world stretched out beneath, it is likely that one is coming from below. Even so, one might be coming from a higher village nearer the Himals, like Torr, in which case the word for come (from below) *kala* will be replaced by the word *yula* come (from above). So I would say on returning from a visit to the schoolmaster's mother in Torr, "Gna Torr ali yula" "I have come from Torr." Most often though, I would make the tone for Torr too soft and high, so the meaning would change and I would have said instead, "I have come from falling down." My inexperience in speaking with tones was a source of great amusement to my friends and family, who roared with laughter as I stood in the house bewildered, having thought I said politely "May I have some water (*ku*, low tone)?" when in fact I had said "May I have a sheep (*ku*, high tone)?" My elder sister, Agai, initially quite skeptical of my presence in the family home, told me early in my stay that I spoke Gurung with the proficiency of her three-year-old son. I was honored, as by my estimation he was by far the better of the two of us.

Tones are a spoken nuance, an inflection that changes meaning. It takes a long time to hear them precisely and longer still to re-create them with your own voice, yet they are simply an unmarked part of life to those who know them, not tones at all, but speech. I listened hard and grasped for them. I struggled from English to Nepali to Gurung in my mind, concentrating, translating, making images into words and words into other words until I felt at a great remove from experience and my head throbbed. Then little by little experience began to come clothed in this new garb. I could speak without thinking (and be understood). The white grains that I wanted on my plate and in my stomach became *bhat* or *kae*, not rice. I thought in Nepali. I dreamed in Nepali. Occasionally an everyday thought would pass through my mind in Gurung. Now I finally lived there.

This process took about six months. During that time I was incompetent at nearly everything. I cried a lot. I wanted to go home. In the first few weeks, every day by evening I would have decided to leave. The children would have teased me. Someone might have turned away from me in mid-sentence because I was hard to understand. A stranger, or worse still a friend or neighbor, might have referred to me as "it." Sample conversation —

Newcomer to villager: "What's that?" (They meant *me*.)

Neighbor: "Who knows? It belongs to Lalita."

Ama might have remonstrated: "Your thighs show when you sit, Ernestine. It embarrasses the men. You must become more modest." I couldn't talk. I couldn't eat. I couldn't sit. I was a nuisance on the trails, poking along behind everyone else while being eaten by the leeches that the warm bodies ahead of me had attracted to the path. When a girl my age snubbed me, I would imagine her in Santa Cruz, totally helpless and lost. When someone said, "She can't talk," I would think angrily, "But I speak English." Just as I was imagining how good I would feel stepping on the plane to California, Ama would bring me some cookies from the tea shop. "I thought my daughter might like these." Or Saras, the tall, gentle woman next door, about my age, would come and sit next to me on the roof of the outhouse (it was easily accessible from the terrace above and had a spectacular view) while I watched the sun set. I could not leave precipitously because it was such a long walk. Vast tracts of land protected me from my rebelliousness, and each decision to leave would be followed by the tugging of my desire to know the place. I wanted to know it, not to give up. Prema lama walked by as I sat outside while night fell. "What are you looking at?" "Clouds." He gave me a piece of candy.

I did learn how to dress. On trips to Cliff Shelter to check my mail at the post office there, I bought glass bangles. Once I had a shiny red blouse made in town and my friends laughed at me, saying I would look like a Brahmin (women of that caste could be recognized by the bright red clothes they wore), and that I must wear the deep, rich maroon and burgundy of the hill people. When winter came, I appreciated the logic of keeping one's clothes on at night and abandoned my nightgowns. People thought it was absurd to have special clothes to sleep in. I did as they did and washed my clothes when I bathed each week, changing into new ones then. Saras showed me how to wash my clothes on rocks and how to bathe in the stream by the small waterfall, washing with my lungi tied up above my breasts, the cold, wet cloth slapping against my body. I became stoic enough not to shriek when we dipped under the icy waterfall to rinse. I liked the routine of draping our wet, clean clothes over bushes to dry, and sitting together on the rocks, quietly combing our hair and looking at the dripping foliage. I looked respectable now, and learned how to weave bright ribbons in my braid. Ama said to me mischievously, "When you go to Cliff Shelter, all the boys will want to sleep with you." She gave me a coral and turquoise necklace to wear, studded with gold, the kind that marks you as a daughter of good family. Each of her other daughters had one. I fingered the cool, smooth beads. Agai, accustomed to me now, twisted strong thread together and restrung it for me with a silver clasp. I wore it even when I slept.

Ama said to me one day, "O Ernestine, when you wear our Gurung clothes, you look entirely Gurung, but when you wear those Japanese clothes, you look quite Japanese."

"What Japanese clothes?"

"You know, the ones from your country."

"Ama, I'm not Japanese. I'm American."

"Japanese, American, it's all the same to me. You look nice in Gurung clothes," she said. I smiled.

I still wear them at home sometimes. They are filled with secrets and memories. The cotton petticoat, hidden underneath ties, with a drawstring. This covers you modestly from waist to feet and provides an anchor for the lungi, the wide tube of bright patterned fabric that you slip on and fold and tuck into the drawstring. My favorite is a soft golden color, with a pattern of vines and large luxuriant pink flowers trailing across it. It belonged to Tson, eventually my close friend, who thought less of it than I did and admired a stiff pink sari of mine with green trim. She suggested a trade and I was delighted. It lies in a drawer in my bedroom now. When you wear a lungi, the pleat should be flat. If you twist it a little as you tuck it in it will hold more firmly. A tight red velvet blouse looks best with this. Then there is the *doro*, seven yards of bright blue cloth that you wrap snugly around your waist, leaving a little pouch at the top where you can put some money or popcorn for a snack. This supports your back and provides a pad for your carrying basket, too. Away from the village women often leave this off because it marks you as a rustic. I also did. Finally there is the maroon velvet shawl, with lines of machine-embroidered flowers. This is very becoming, and makes up the necessary *pardah*, or veil.

I did not realize this for a long time, until I went out one day, and a woman noticed me leaving and said, "Don't forget your shawl."

"I won't need it," I said. "It's terrifically hot."

"To go out without a shawl is a matter of shame," she replied, "It is your pardah." I was puzzled, having only heard the term in reference to a curtain. Was I a window or a doorway?

"Here," she said, "Take a light one. And you don't need to wrap it. Just drape it over your shoulder, like so. Then people will know you are modest."

I learned the value of veils, to wrap when you want to withdraw, to flirt with a smile and then drape the cloth over head and shoulders to show you were not improper, to stand pressed against one's friends in a crowd, neatly wrapped and filled with wicked comments, like the young girls who said to the old Brahmin fruit peddler that his guavas were likely as withered as his balls, then flicked their veils properly over their shoulders and walked away. The maroon velvet shawl also shows that you are Gurung, because they come from Hong Kong and Gurung men in the Gurkhas bring them back and give them as gifts to their relatives. I wanted one for a long time. I bought mine from a woman in the village. My friend Leela said it looked a little old and I might have paid too much for it. I only minded a little and was glad to feel its softness wrapped around me.

"Ah," said people in the town, "you must live with Gurungs."

"Yes," I said, "I do."

everyday lifes
soul & body

3.
The Fate of Embodied Beings

As words shape your thoughts, clothes shape your body. So do houses and beds and chairs or mats and the company you keep. You will trip over a lungi if your weight is not held back a little, or if your legs are stiff when you walk. In Gurung villages, doorways are low, so you have to bow a little as you enter a house. The beds and mats are hard; you cannot sink into them. People's bodies are contained, arms and legs held close to the trunk, so that large untidy gestures seem out of place. My body changes in Nepal. As I stayed there, my center of balance shifted lower. This made me more stable going up and down trails and helped me move more effectively in a lungi or sari. I also became more erect. Carrying loads strapped to my head strengthened me, and when a bundle of grass or a pot of water was removed, I felt my whole body rise upward, so light I could float. Physically I began to fit in well enough that twice people on the trails mistook me for a Brahmin girl (the more round-eyed caste), arguing with one another, once coming back for a second look, then pronouncing confidently that I was certainly not a Westerner but surely a Brahmin. I was flattered and my friends were amused.

Many things we think of without form have bodies in Nepal: gods, ancestors, evil spirits, uncanny creatures, dead people (whose human bodies have been cremated). These must be tended: placated, pleased, or cajoled with offerings. Bonds are conceived as physical. "I love Seyli because she is my daughter," said Ama, no special qualities noted or needed, just the fact of kinship. I was not related by blood but was offered up by fate, a "dharma daughter." Once given, this relationship, too, needed tending.

Ama's affection drew me into a large net of relations. I sometimes felt like I was caught in a sticky web, not sure how to proceed, wishing for more freedom than I had, or at least for more understanding. Once I was documenting the naming ceremony of Tson's newborn son. The old lama from across the gorge chanted as dim light filtered through the fretted window, illuminating the smoke that hung in the air and casting small square shadows on the floor. Tson held the baby Ratna and relatives sat around on the wooden cots by the walls, watching and chatting a little.

"Go get water, Ernestine," said Ama. The stream was half a mile away, at the top of the village and around a bend into the jungle. Filling the five-gallon jug could take a while, especially if there were others in line.

"But Ama, I am writing down this ritual."

"Go get water, Ernestine." On goes the headstrap, the basket on the back, the thump of the copper water pot. Step, step, step, up the path. By the time I got back, the ceremony was over. Still, it is clear to me now that the value of the credit I got among people as a dutiful daughter far outweighed the benefits that might have been conferred by witnessing the ritual.

Another time six or seven young men and women came to my room to visit and chat, and talked on and on into the night.

"I am ready to sleep now," I said.

"Fine," replied Radha from next door. "You go right ahead. It won't bother us at all."

"Well," I said, being in my ignorance horrifically rude, "I don't think I can go to sleep with my room full of people." People thought it odd that I slept in a room by myself. In the big house, Tson slept with one of the little girls and later with her baby. Ama or Bunti slept with the other daughter. Apa and Maila might sleep alone, but the room was filled with mats unrolled on the floor and sleeping alone meant you were only a few feet from someone. Now and then Ama would say, "O Ernestine, come sleep in the house with me tonight." We would curl up on the narrow cot together and after I had finally dozed off, someone would light the small kerosene lamp and say, "Is anyone else awake?" Words would be exchanged among bundled bodies on the mats. Someone else might say, "I am going for a pee. Does anyone else want to come?" The door opens, more conversation follows. The door closes. "Did you bolt the door?" Finally the light goes out. A few more words, finally silence. I drift back into sleep, but soon, a little before dawn, the mats are rolled up, the door is opened. Tson begins to make the tea. I feel stiff all over and wretchedly tired.

There, the proper place for bodies is together. From infancy a child is in the midst of people, enveloped by social life. No one is quiet for a sleeping baby, it simply learns to adjust to the sounds and activities of other humans, and after three weeks or so of irritable crying when disturbed, it is not disturbed anymore. Perhaps the rustle and talk of human life weave into its dreams. I was too old to adjust to that, and needed the womb of my room to sleep soundly and be born refreshed again into their world. For my friends there, the expressions "There was a huge crowd" or "There was a crush of people" indicated that an event was truly wonderful. Because I lived at the headman's house, there were always people in and out and about. It was the central meeting place of the village.

"Don't you ever want to be alone?" I asked Tson.

"I sometimes *am* alone," she replied, "Like if I am cooking and everyone else is out in the fields. If that happens, I don't mind. But I don't seek to be alone. I don't understand why anyone would *want* to be alone."

She continued to chop the potatoes and handed me one to cut. A large round pot of rice bubbled on the flames. "At my home in Torr," she said, "my family was stricter about separating us during our monthly periods, and I went to the small room above the stable and slept alone there when it came. I liked that. It was peaceful. I felt clean. Here when a woman has her period no one seems to care at all. You can cook and touch anything except the altar. It mixes everything up and is not very restful or correct. My brother is a lama and our household was strict about religious things."

"I thought concern about women's periods was a Hindu sort of thing, not Buddhist," I said.

"It is all religion. Do you wash your hair after your period?" she asked.

"No," I answered, "I didn't know I was supposed to do that."

"That's all right," she said. "Buddha forgives errors commited in ignorance. You should do it from now on, though. If it's cold outside just put a little soap on some hair in the middle of your forehead, rub it and say, 'purity, purity.' That will be enough." She sighed. "Your mother makes me do all the cooking here. If I'm not cooking, I have to go chop wood. Even if I feel sick and dizzy because of the baby inside me, I have to work. It is rude to lie down in front of your in-laws; it is bad to complain. I never get to rest. It was nice at my home. I could do whatever I liked there."

"Is it better when your husband is here?" I asked.

She blushed. "No. He bothers me. For three years, when I first came here, if he came into the house, I would go out. I would not even look at him. I never spoke to him. I missed my home then and I miss my home now." She blew a stray piece of hair out of her face and dropped the potato pieces into the pot.

I had been to Tson's home. She was from Torr. Many marriages took place between families in the two villages, Tebas and Torr. Marriage is the weaving of the net of relationship, drawing out women like threads to connect two lineages. Apa's sister, Pajon, had grown up in Tebas and married in Torr. Growing up, Ama had spent time in both villages, but her lineage was based in Torr and she had married in Tebas. It was considered good to take a bride from the place from which your mother had come, as this could be the basis of a bond of affection and loyalty in the sometimes tense relationship between mother-in-law and daughter-in-law. It was especially good if she came from the same lineage, repeating and strengthening connections. Tson did not come from the same lineage as Ama, but she was from a very respectable family in the same village. She was an exemplary daughter-in-law: modest, hardworking, and, as she noted, uncomplaining, at least to elders. Her brother, the lama, had a wife and two children and lived in the family home with his mother. Their father, now dead, had also been a lama. Their house was in a hamlet of Torr called Lower Village, overlooking terraced fields so high and steep that you could not see the river below. The gorge was narrow and the other side seemed close and was so rugged that it was not terraced at all. The craggy Himals were near, huge and white at the gorge's end, and when the wind rushed through it was icy. From their courtyard in the other direction, you could see a path winding up along the side of the mountain as it entered the village. Their house was large and quiet, less topsy-turvy and filled with people than the house in Tebas, and their courtyard was a little apart from others, surrounded by a low wall, with a stable in the corner, a red-windowed room above it. There was a feeling of peace and spaciousness about the place. Her mother was quiet and sweet, and held my hand when she spoke with me. I could see why Tson cherished the rare chance to come home for a visit.

Tson had been married when she was thirteen, a young girl with long, thick hair. Her hair was very black, her skin smooth and her mouth small and full. Her large dark eyes were set a little close to each other, and she had a direct look that was endearing. She told me she had been standing on the wall at the edge of the courtyard combing her hair, when she had seen the marriage procession coming in the distance: the groom and his male relatives in turbans, the important men of their village accompanying them. Among Gurungs then, girls were not told of their marriages. Parents arranged the marriage, and a boy might be given his choice out of four or five pre-selected possibilities, but the girl was not even told of the arrangements. For a girl to express liking for any boy would be shameful, so there were no questions to be posed. And a girl who knew she was to be wrenched from her home and sent to live with strangers would likely run off, hoping to hide until the time the priests had deemed auspicious for the wedding had passed, or until they wearied of looking for her, or until her prospective in-laws decided that such a recalcitrant daughter-in-law was not for them. Usually, though, they were hunted down, dragged back, and the wedding proceeded as planned. Girls worried as they reached adolescence, knowing that any day a party of men might come to the house to take them.

Tson stood there watching, and said to her mother, "Look, a marriage party. I wonder who they are coming for?"

"Hush," said her mother. "It is for your cousin but if you say anything, they will take you instead."

It was April, when the red rhododendron flowers bloom in the high forest above Torr, great rhododendron trees, whose branches reach out, intertwine, and cover the sky. The blossoms drop and carpet the forest floor. Tson stood on the ledge with the tall white mountains behind her, quietly combing her hair. She said the older men who reached the courtyard first had tears on their cheeks, seeing her standing there so innocent. Her groom was eighteen, turbaned and strange. They lifted her, to carry her back to Tebas, and she wept and cried for her mother.

"It is your marriage, my daughter," she said. "You must go." The mother also wept. Trumpets and drums, the triumphant celebration of men, drowned Tson's sobs and she was brought to her husband's house, dressed in finery and given as his bride. Animals were sacrificed and all the village came for the feasting.

A bride is not immediately made a wife. When a girl is married young, the marriage may not be consummated for a long time, even years, and it is considered better not to force the bride. Girls go home to visit for long periods at first, becoming accustomed little by little to the ways of the new place. Tson said that for the first few years in Tebas, she insisted on continuing to sleep with his sister when her husband was home on leave from India, resisting the coaxing and strategies of the family. Then one night the sister went out after Tson had settled down and was replaced by her husband, who seeing her shocked look, said gently, "I am nothing fearsome. Look, I'm not a leopard come to hurt you." By that night, she was in her late teens, now a wife and soon to be a mother, and her restful visits home were only occasional.

*   *   *

Tson and I sat in the courtyard together combing our hair when she told me that story. Our knees touched. We oiled and combed with small bamboo combs from Amrit Kumari's shop, and braided our hair. It was years later, when I had returned to Nepal. She had four sons, and was in her early thirties, as was I. She was back briefly, her husband's leave nearly at an end. She stayed with him in India now. Tson, who when I had suggested that she accompany me for a day in Cliff Shelter years before, had replied, "Who do I know in Cliff Shelter that I should go there?" She had, at that time, never descended the mountain on which we lived, having gone only from one side of it to the other, from Torr to Tebas. Now she lived in India. There had been a property division among the sons, and it had gone badly for Tson and her husband, as Maila's wife, a greedy woman with ambitions to live in the city, had pressed for land they should have shared. "That's all right," said Tson. "It was not worth quarreling over. My husband and I both agreed. We are alike, you know, simple, with hearts like children. We did not want to quarrel over property." She spoke warmly of the ways he cared for her and said, "We will be fine." She took my hand.

"Your hands are so soft and smooth," she said.

"I use lotion from America. Would you like some?"

"Your hands are soft because you do not work like we do. See." She showed me the callouses on her hand that had made them hard. I remembered years before at meals when I could not lift my hot brass bowl of food to pour the curry on the rice, she would laugh at me and take it up and pour it, like she did for the children, those callouses protecting her from the heat. "You still look like a young girl," she said. I did not work outside. I had no children. She looked beautiful to me. Knowing that she had been living in India, I had not expected to see her on that trip. To be sitting there together in the courtyard felt like a miracle. "When I arranged gifts for everyone, I did not know you would be here," she said. I had brought a smooth knit blouse to leave for her. Gifts are always given when you come from far away. "When we meet again, I will give you a shawl," she said. "They have nice ones in India. What color would you like?"

"I think a green one."

"I will bring a lovely green one for you, then, when we meet again."

*   *   *

Tson and I were close in the way of family, without the polite distance of friends who tend to see one's better self, smoothed and refined for public viewing. As an intimate of the household and someone my age, when she was nineteen and I twenty-one, she had witnessed all my fits of petulance and rage. There were always people coming to my room and going through my things, inspecting them and asking questions, requesting items large and small, wanting to watch while I typed my notes, to listen to a tape recording one more time, to look at my hair or my skin close up; "Look, she has hair on her arm like an animal," someone once said. All these were usual things to do and not ill intended, but I often lost patience and asked people to leave my room or said flatly, "No," to a request by a lively young woman or a sweet old man, or lost my temper with the children and shouted at them. These were not usual things to do and were seen as very ill mannered. I could also be sullen and demanding around the house. "We try to convince people you are a nice person," Tson said to me once in exasperation, "But you don't make it easy." She had been there, too, when I was washed away by waves of homesick sadness, feeling lost and alone, sobbing in my room. She and Saras came in and held me, telling me to hush lest everyone come to watch. (Displays of emotion generally drew a crowd.) Saras said that during her time in India with her husband, she had cried too, tired of feeling strange and lonely, missing the mountains and her home. "Don't cry, don't cry," they said, stroking my hair. I felt better, wiped my face with a corner of my lungi, and sat out in the sun with them for a while.

I had seen Tson's quiet resentment at being heaped with household tasks by Ama and the luminous sweetness with which she sang prayers as she lit the altar lamp in the evening. I had worked with her around the hearth and in the fields and forest, just a little, feeling rather like Marie Antoinette playing shepherdess at Versailles. People were always solicitous of me, worried that I would hurt myself doing work to which they were long accustomed and I was not at all. I had proven my ability to carry and was a cheerful beast of burden, so I was happily given loads, but when I went out with Tson, Saras, and Radha to help them cut wood, they would not allow me to use the small ax lest I cut myself. I shared the snacks and company and carried a basket of wood home, but sat among the ferns and looked at the forest while they chopped.

When Tson gave birth to her first son in the spring of my first year in Tebas, I learned how raw little morsels of life were brought up to be people. I had gone down to Cliff Shelter to check my mail at the post office there, staying overnight at the welcoming inn of a Thakali family, traders from the north who had settled there. Cliff Shelter was a small bazaar on the main trail. The trail eased into it from a meadow past a large waterfall, whose low roar could be heard from the forest above it. As you turned the bend, the path widened into a flagstone street, lined by open shops and the wide verandas of the inns. There was a small, plain temple by the river, a little red and white structure with a bell. Cliff Shelter consisted of maybe twenty houses, inns and shops where the families slept upstairs and wares were sold below. The river wound round it on three sides. I would sleep hearing the rushing water and wake to the bells of the mule caravans. I might write some letters in the afternoon, chat with the family or talk with tourists in the evening, English feeling strange in my mouth, and stop at the bangle shop on the way back for some new glass bangles and a ribbon or two. I was nothing remarkable in Cliff Shelter, a mainly Thakali community whose inhabitants were more cosmopolitan than the villagers and who had plenty of Western trekkers to observe. In contrast to other foreigners, I was like another kid from the neighborhood, useful in translating tourists' requests. I liked the combination of freedom and belonging and came for a day or two every couple of weeks. The father of the family who owned the inn I stayed at, Bhimsen, was a wise and kind man frequently called on by locals to settle disputes. His sensitive advice often helped me to understand and untangle confusing situations back in Tebas.

The walk from Cliff Shelter took four or five hours, and I got back to Tebas at evening, as the sun was going down over the mountain across the gorge. Our village caught the last evening light. I entered the house through the double doors, always open unless the family was away or asleep.

"You've come," said Ama. This was the usual greeting, whether one had come from the next village or Hong Kong. I saw Tson lying on a mat by the fire, a tiny infant tucked up next to her. Excited, I lay my hand on her leg.

"Oh Tson, your baby was born!" She smiled.

Ama flicked several drops of holy water from the altar at me, and said, "You must not touch your Tson now. For three days after birth, a woman is untouchable, impure." The holy water neutralized the impurity. I moved back a little. "Then for eleven days she should lie down," said Ama. "And for thirty days she should not work, though some resume work sooner."

Agai came to visit and she and other women throughout the village each brought a shawl and a chicken. I, too, walked up from Amrit Kumari's shop with some cloth and a chicken dangled upside down by its feet, lulled into calm by the rhythm of my steady steps. The gift of cloth helps anchor the new mother's souls in her body. Otherwise the shock and disruption of giving birth might dislodge some of them (women have seven souls, it is believed, and men have nine) and the woman would fall ill. The chickens are to provide the rich broth that a new mother must have in order to build her strength. Women of the lineage are obliged to make these gifts, but others also brought them for Tson because she was the daughter-in-law of a prominent household, and because she was well liked.

People do not simply hold together there, in their belief. We share that idea, really, though it is more muted, in the concept that under stress we can "fall apart" or "go to pieces" and that through "support" we may be made whole again. For Gurungs, the possiblity of disintegration is ever present. The self is unstable and even a small shock, like stumbling over a rock on the trail, can cause one's souls to fly out. To lose a soul is to become unwell, to lose them all is to die. Social life restores the souls: the gift on large occasions of disruption or distress, like birth, bereavement, or misfortune; a thread tied around your neck by a mother or sister when you are ill, accompanied by the phrase *shah, shah* whose soft, breathy sound catches the soul and keeps it in place; the phrase is invoked again when you stumble, by friends who will stroke your head and shoulders, calming you and containing your souls, the *plah*.

Babies and young children are volatile, barely here, their lives only tentatively established. Everything is new and strange and their souls are not well anchored. Many die in the village: an infection, a stomach upset, or just a sad morning when you wake to find your child gone, its empty body left behind, *syi yae*, "gone to death." Ama had ten children and lost three. Atay, her husband's elder brother's wife, had fifteen and lost eight. The little ones are mourned by their parents but no full public funeral takes place; a child does not belong to the community in that way until it has its permanent front teeth. This is a household grief. "That was his destiny," the neighbors will say, the law of karma playing itself out; the parents' destiny, too, to lose the child.

Ratna, Tson's son, was robust and grew up well. His souls were encouraged to stay in place by warm massages near the fire, believed also to help the body develop properly. Several times a day Tson would place him on a blanket on the hearth, a heated dish of clarified butter nearby and rub his limbs, torso, head, genitals with her hands, warming her fingers over the coals. I loved to see his slippery golden skin and plump limbs and the relaxed, absorbed look on his face. Ama said I watched with greedy eyes and concluded, "You want a baby, too." He eagerly drank his mother's milk, abundant enough that she offered it to a tiny Brahmin baby whose mother had none, who would gratefully bring him from another village to the house several times a day, saving his life by giving him Tson's good nourishment.

I carried water and grass, helping old women as they came with their buffaloes' fodder piled high in baskets, sat in the courtyards and talked with people, retiring to my room to write down the events of the day before the light began to fade. If I came down to warm my hands in the afternoon sun and was tempted by a conversation in the courtyard, Ama would say, "Just stay until your hands are warm and then go back to your writing. You must forge a reputation with your work, do it with honor." Honor was paramount to her. "We used to be one of the richest families around," she once told me, "We had a great deal of land and cash when it was rare. Now with many children we are not so wealthy. Still, we are among the most honorable. Lesser people have become Gurkha officers and richer than we are. They like to pretend to be big and make us small. But they cannot touch us. We have our honor." To have many children is honorable, yet they consume the wealth that maintains honor. Land and gold mark honor, yet as they are divided and passed down they dwindle. Honor is passed through blood and bone. It is physical, inherited, essential, yet it must be enacted to be socially real, through gifts and hospitality, through power and ownership. It is inherited, yet must be cultivated. It is essential, yet can be lost.

Although their household was wealthy in village terms, Ama worried about money. Atay, who lived in the other great house of their lineage, married to Apa's brother Badhay, felt secure. "My father had known his father in the army," said Atay. "They were friends and so they arranged our marriage." She was from Panglo, a village built on a high ridge overlooking the river, beautiful and stark, and constantly assaulted by icy winds there on its outcropping. "My father had honor and our house was wealthy. I came from wealth and married into wealth."

"There was lots of land then?" I asked.

"Lots of land then and lots of land now," she answered. "And the trees were so abundant we needed only to step out of the courtyard to get wood for the fire or fodder for the animals."

"Even with five sons there is enough now for all?" I asked.

"Even with five sons there is plenty," she replied. Atay was in her sixties. She was gray and missing several teeth, but was erect and dignified. She had a warm, direct cheerfulness and was easy on her daughters-in-law. "My mother-in-law said 'Work when you want to. Rest when you want to.' It was easy and I was happy here," Atay told me. She seemed to follow this principle and Radha and Saras, her daughters-in-law, were respectful and affectionate with her. Radha's husband, Ram, had forgone a military career to farm and to care for his aging parents, and his brother, Lakshman, married to Saras, was away in the Indian army. An unmarried brother, Gopal, was home on leave from India. The other sons were away in the army and the daughters were married, one in Torr and one in Tebas. Years later after Atay had died, when the property was divided among the sons, there proved not to be enough to sustain a living through the land. The brothers in the military were all right, but Ram and Radha struggled and, between gifts from their uncles, their children sometimes wore threadbare clothes. Though they still had honor, it helped them only a little.

Ama had only three sons and a larger portion of land, since her father had included property in the gift he had made to her at marriage, but she was concerned that her children might need more to protect their well-being and their honor than they would get. I gave money each month for my room and board. "A gift," Ama had said, "whatever you want to give. I cannot charge rent to a daughter."

When we went to the tea shop or traveled together, I paid, and in insecure moments, the words that Amrit Kumari had uttered in a bad mood rang in my ears: "She does not love you at all. She just wants you there for your money. She doesn't love anyone. All she cares about is money." Amrit Kumari said the amount I gave monthly was extravagant. "You could rent a room in town for that." When an egg or a glass of milk would be there in the house for a son but not for me, though I might be just over an illness and in need of nourishment and strength, I would wonder if Amrit Kumari were right, but later, when I felt better and was happy again with the usual diet of potatoes and rice, I would realize I was truly being treated like a daughter of the family. Only the sons were ever given strengthening treats.

When Ama would look at shoes I seldom wore and say, "You know, Saila could use some shoes like that. They are about his size. Will you give them to him?" Again I would wonder. Then I would see around me that request was a language of relationship. I noticed that friends commonly asked such things of each other.

After Agai, the eldest sister, had finally came to like me, we were sitting in my room once talking and she saw a simple blue blouse I had lying out and asked me for it. I gave it to her and, a little confused, asked Amrit Kumari what Agai might have meant by that. Being then in a more benign mood, she said, "It means she cares for you and wants to have something of yours. It means she feels close to you and now you can ask her for things, too."

Ama requested things of me from time to time and clearly appreciated the money I brought to the household. She did care a great deal about money, as Amrit Kumari and others noted. Times were changing; life was insecure, and honor needed wealth to make it real and effective. Wealth was no doubt part of her attraction to having me in the house, but I think she felt, like me, a strange connection when we met that remained between us, sometimes tenuous, sometimes stronger. Besides, as Pajon said when she sent me from Torr, "Lalita always likes something new and interesting."

In the West, we tend to think of motives as clear and singular even though we know their tangled complexity. "Why did she do that?" we will ask, as though there were a single answer, a note rather than a chord determining behavior.

"A person should be nice to everyone," said our neighbor Leela, "because you never know whose help you will need." Yet, far from being instrumental, she was consistently warm and generous, taking sole responsibility for her elderly and frail father-in-law who preferred her care to that of his other son's wife, a cooler and more perfunctory caretaker. She made sure that the workers who came from the untouchable hamlet at the edge of the village had occasional gifts as well as their wages. She shared food with neighbors, and constantly invited me for tea, saying playfully, "It has been three days since I have seen your face. You must not neglect us. Come after breakfast and sit with me a while." All of us were people quite unlikely to be able to offer her help. Her generosity was not modulated according to anyone's use-value, yet it was informed by this pragmatic sense, an attention to the practical necessity of giving and taking in the world in which she lived.

This was very different from what I had known, growing up in a place where pragmatism and feeling were considered so separate as to contaminate each other, where one could not say, "She is kind to you because she thinks you might be useful to her one day," without calling real affection into question. I was pragmatically useful to Ama, and I think she loved me. Though I had no practical goals at that time of obtaining a professional credential or an advanced degree, coming with more diffuse and insidious personal ambitions to understand something like the meaning of life, Ama offered me essential pragmatic assistance, providing the home, the training, the base of information needed to live in that world. I loved her, too. In the end Saila did not like my shoes, so Apa wore them.

In Tebas, feelings and practicality, ideas and bodies intermingled. To love someone because you were dependent on them or might have something to gain was not necessarily to love them less. To desire honor was not to long just for something abstract, the opinions or judgments of others, but to want a life condition, a value that placed you beyond criticism and contributed to an inner strength and stability that offered protection from physical harm and illness.

Leela came from an honorable lineage in Torr and married in Tebas. She was fair with high cheekbones and a very pretty face, a little plump. Her intelligence showed in her eyes. She was strong but open-hearted, and I first got to know her when she translated the bantering remarks of other young wives from Gurung into Nepali for me.

"Why did you tell her that?" said one young woman indignantly after making a very funny ribald remark.

"She might want to laugh, too," said Leela.

Her mother-in-law was dead and her husband was in Hong Kong with the British army. He, too, had a lively intelligence and when home on leave talked about relationships in *Hamlet* and their resemblance to village life with a sweet and eager unpretentiousness. Leela lived with her father-in-law and two-year-old daughter in a house a few terraces away from ours. Her father-in-law was a tall spindly old man with bony knees, who spent most of the day on a mat in the sun, and sometimes carried his small granddaughter about. He, too, had been a soldier and had fought in Europe in World War I. He called me "child" and when I gave him a course of antibiotics for a respiratory infection, delivering each pill at the proper time each day, he told people I was a goddess who had saved his life. Then he would declaim the blessings of a father to a child: "May you be honorable. May you marry a colonel or a general. May you be well." From child to deity to child, I went. In Nepal, deities need offerings. Dispensing boons, they are dependent on human care, part of the cycle of giving and taking. Everyone has god within. Anyone might be a goddess. Elders are like gods and their blessings bring good. I bowed when the old man gave me blessings and felt happy and safe standing in the sun in their courtyard. There was a general sweetness about the household and I liked to spend time there, appreciating their good company and the serene quiet of their corner of the village.

Leela and her husband had others sharecrop their land, so she was mainly around the house and courtyard during the day, and liked me to stop by when I could. Like Tson, she had never seen her husband before their marriage. She said his uncle had known her as a child when she was living in the military compound in Hong Kong with her father. He came often to visit and had given her candy. She called him "candy uncle."

On their return, when she was eleven, her husband's uncle came with her future father-in-law to request a betrothal. She excitedly announced that "candy uncle" had arrived and was disappointed to be sent out of the room while the grownups talked. Her parents agreed to the proposal, deferring the marriage until she was older. She had been out of earshot, but her younger sister overheard the conversation and rushed to tell her that her parents had agreed to give her away to that family. Leela told me, "I thought I was to be sent to be a servant in their house, and I went to my mother and cried. 'No,' she said, 'it's your marriage. All women have to leave their homes. Your father's sister went, and I came here and had you. We all have to go.'"

Leela told me she still felt sad after that, and cried from time to time at the thought of being sent from her home. "Now I am here," she said. "And it is not bad, though I did not want to leave my home. But a woman's life is hard. Pregnancy is difficult. You feel sick and get headaches. Birth is frightening. If the baby or the placenta does not come, you die. I thought when I married, 'I do not want to have daughters, only sons,' because a daughter's life is full of suffering. Now I have this little girl, but I hope all my other children will be sons." She had five daughters as time went on and wept, I was told, when she held the fifth one in her arms.

Leela was robust and attractive. Cheerful and healthy, she said, "I am strong because I do not worry, thinking 'What about this? What about that?' To worry makes your heart-mind small." Nursing her child, she explained to me that when your heart-mind contracts you become weak, sad, and vulnerable to illness; when it is large and expansive, you are confident, optimistic, strong. Worry, grief, rejection, shame all cause it to contract. Peace, joy, belonging, honor all cause it to expand.

This heart-mind, the *sae*, is located in the center of the chest and is the seat of feeling, memory, and of consciousness, so to say a person has fainted is: "Her heart-mind went into forgetfulness." The heart-mind is not a philosophical concept, but a day to day reality: one goes looking for a memory and finds that it is "not in the heart-mind"; one is wounded by a friend and the "heart-mind hurts"; one is reunited with a loved one and there is "happiness in the heart-mind." To have a large heart-mind is to be responsive to others and generous. To have a small heart-mind is to be self-absorbed and stingy. With a small heart-mind, worries "eat the heart-mind"; anger comes easily; strength dissipates—spiritual strength diminishing so that one attracts accidents and misfortune and falls prey to malevolent forces, physical strength diminishing so that one falls ill. A calm stability keeps the heart-mind strong. Leela exemplified the virtues of a large heart-mind and experienced its benefits.

The heart-mind is one of those beliefs that knits the person and the world together. We have such beliefs, too, in the West, but they are more diffuse because we see ourselves as more separate and contained as persons. In the West, we focus more on individuality than on connection. We do not seem to ourselves volatile, flying apart when startled, stressed or shocked, held together (literally) by the attentions of others, as expressed in Gurung ideas about the *plah* or souls. In the West, persons imagine themselves to be more bounded. Ideas of unstable souls show how strongly reactive Gurungs conceive themselves to be and how much they depend on others to maintain wholeness.

Ideas of the *sae* or heart-mind reveal other understandings about the person; like those about the souls, they too differ from concepts in the West. The "mind" for Westerners is more abstract, less physically experienced, less modified by the pain and pleasure we encounter in life. It is usually conceived without dimensions, though there are some parallels and we too can be "small-minded" or "great-hearted." The heart-mind brings feeling, memory, and thought together in the body. In this place at the center of the chest, life in the world penetrates and modifies the inner self. The modified self then attracts certain experiences and repels others. Yet the person is not just passively molded by the world. One can "make the heart-mind strong" when faced with temptation or "make the heart-mind bright" when suffering. These efforts of will protect the expanse of the heart-mind, even when it is being assaulted by diminishing experiences. The care and sustenance of others helps in this. The heart-mind implicates one in life, deeply and moment to moment. It shows how the world shapes people and how they, in their responses, condition circumstances. It shows how involvement in others' lives affects our deepest selves and theirs.

On the terrace below Leela's, to the south side of the village where houses were sheltered by the curve of the hill, a little off to the side of the main path (so less traversed by foot traffic and buffaloes on their way to pasture) there were three smaller houses belonging to less prominent members of the village. One was a small round dwelling with a thatched roof, nudged into the angle between the terrace behind and the hill at the side, grassy tufts and spindly bushes sticking out of the slope. Instead of a flagstone courtyard, it had flat porch. There was no raised veranda as on the larger village houses. It was a very old-style house, of the kind common half a century and more before, when Gurungs had occupied themselves mainly with herding and shifted households from summer to winter pastures. It was a circle made of mud over a wooden frame, low with only one story, smoky with a wide doorway but no window. A small pile of wood was stacked neatly next to it, and it was dim inside. It was inhabited by an old widow named Mallum whose one daughter was married and gone. Her clothes were old and worn. She was often busy caring for her small farming plot or gathering firewood, stooped under a load of sticks. She sometimes stopped by her neighbors' courtyards to visit, but people seldom called out to her to chat, because she tended to be gloomy, often complaining, finding fault, and predicting that someone or another's plan would come to nothing, or worse.

Closer to the path on a more open site were two stone houses. These were joined, separate homes that shared one wall and the veranda, a kind of village duplex. Small houses were often built in that style and often belonged, like these, to brothers. They were a modest family, without clan titles, large landholdings, or impressive military rank. The older brother had married out of caste, which had lowered their lineage in the esteem of others. His wife's caste was respectable but not to marry a Gurung was to muddle up the proper order of things and caused considerable loss of status. Not only that, but the wife was coarse and outspoken, downed large amounts of liquor at festivals, and flirted openly with other men, definite liabilities to the family. The younger brother was a gentle, soft-spoken man whose wife had died some years before. He had two daughters in their late teens, Rita and Mina. They were both very pretty, vivacious and playful. The youngest, Mina, was quite beautiful by any standard and was very well liked for her warmth and outrageous sense of humor. Rita, the older sister was more serious, having had to take over the running of the household and supervision of her sister at an early age, but she too had a lovely insouciant streak. A boy from the headman's lineage had asked permission of Apa to marry Rita, having gotten to know her around the village and come to love her, but he had been refused on account of their lower status and the out of caste marriage. His marriage was arranged with another girl, and Rita remained unmarried.

Rita and Mina often stopped by Leela's courtyard and would join us sitting on mats in the sun with Leela's little girl. She would offer them tea and snacks and they would play with the baby or help stack the firewood and tell us about their day. They were close friends with Bunti, so I often saw them at our house, preparing to go into the forest together to find fodder for the animals or cut wood, talking and laughing as they gathered their baskets and scythes. The more outgoing Mina always made it a point to call out to me when I passed and addressed me warmly as "elder sister" when with her friends, a pack of teenage girls who, rendered uneasy by my strangeness, could be quite stand-offish.

My last conversation with her had been when I was walking past her family's fields on my way home from Cliff Shelter. She was wearing a cherry-red velvet blouse that set off her dark hair and eyes and she laughed with me in the sun as she harvested millet, cutting the stiff brown stalks with her curved sickle. For some time after that I did not see her.

Then when I stopped by to visit Leela, she said, "Did you know Mina has been sick?"

"No," I replied. "I had no idea."

"It has been about two weeks. She seems to be getting worse each day."

Later I asked Bunti and Ama about her illness. Bunti said she had become weak and sick to her stomach, but had continued to work in the fields because the millet needed to be brought in. Then the fever came on and got stronger and she had to go to bed. "Go see her," she said. While I had chatted with her on the path by her house, I had never been inside and barely knew her family. I felt shy, but I went the next day.

Their house was small. When I came in, Rita greeted me. It took me a moment to become accustomed to the dim light inside after the afternoon sun. Her father was there, along with an older man and woman, more distant relatives from a different part of the village. The shaman was just leaving. "He has been blowing mantras into her body," said the old woman, "to chase out the sickness." Mina lay on the cot by the fire. She was wearing the same cherry-red blouse I had seen on her in the fields. Everything else was different. Her eyes were half closed and her skin was dull and dry. Her body lay limply and she babbled a steady stream of words, not looking around, never stopping. She was saying something about millet. "Hush," said the old woman. "We'll take care of the millet." I felt a sinking feeling in my stomach and an undertow of sadness. I sat on the edge of her cot and touched her arm. It was hot.

"Mina," I said.

There was a pause in her babbling. "Elder sister?"

Her father looked up. "She knows you," he said. "She has not recognized anyone all day." He looked excited and hopeful, but she took no more notice of me and slipped back down into her stream of words, lost to us again, like Ophelia sinking in the river. Her father stood near, wanting to sit by her. I moved.

"I have some medicine," I said. I had an all-purpose medical kit with a range of remedies for endemic illnesses and a medical manual from the Peace Corps describing local diseases and the symptoms they manifest, matching symptoms, disease, and treatment like a children's puzzle. The course of Mina's illness matched typhoid fever.

"We tried your kind of treatment and it didn't work," he said. "The pharmacist below the village gave us two capsules, but they did nothing." "Capsules" were tetracycline.

"You need more than two," I said. "You need to give them every day."

"The pharmacist said two were enough," replied her father. "She is too weak for such strong medicine now." I looked at the floor, the clay a little dusty from people going in and out. The old woman was dribbling water into Mina's mouth with a spoon.

"Do you know of anything else we could do?" asked the old man.

"No," I replied. "I am not a doctor. I think it is good to give her water." I walked out into the courtyard. Ears of corn were stacked on a tall rack drying. I squinted in the light. Everything seemed bright, almost lurid. I walked home slowly, looking at the flagstones, my mouth feeling dry. By the time I reached the gateway of our courtyard, I felt stronger, less wobbly. Our household seemed secure and welcoming. Ama sat by the fire with Kanchi, while Tson nursed her baby and stirred the tea. Small potatoes for snacks lay roasting under the coals. I sat on the mat near Ama.

"I went to see Mina," I said. "She is very sick."

"Yes," she answered, "so I have heard. If it is written in her destiny to live, she will live. If it is not, she will die."

The goddess of destiny writes a child's fate on its forehead when it is six days old, according to what the karma accrued in previous lifetimes decrees. I thought of her lying in the shadows on the cot, and wondered what her destiny would be.

*　*　*

Some months before, I had been staying with Pajon, Apa's sister and the schoolmaster's mother, in Torr. I had come to see the *pae*, the memorial celebration performed anywhere from a few weeks to several months after a death, depending on when the bereaved family can get sufficient money together to pay for the feasting and the priests. The *pae* frees the spirit from wandering in limbo and sends it to the afterlife. Usually the officiating priests are Buddhist lamas whose main task is to chant the Tibetan Book of the Dead and to dance around the effigy of the deceased at twilight each evening. The ultimate Gurung ritual, it lasts three days and two nights, and on the final evening, a canopy covering the effigy is pulled back and the spirit is released to the chanting and drumming of the priests and the sobbing and keening of the mourners. This is what I had come to study. In Torr this time, the ritual was to be performed by the shamans of the village, renowned in the area for their skill. They were three brothers in their fifties and sixties, with straight bodies and lined faces, quiet and direct in bearing. The ritual was for their own brother and mother. Unlike the Buddhist lamas, the shamans did not use a text, but recited ancient chants. "Old Buddhism," they called it. The lamas said it was not Buddhism at all. The shamans practiced the old religion of Tibet, there before lamaic Buddhism arrived. Like the lamas, they called the spirit to come and inhabit the effigy, a structure set in front of the house in which the deceased had lived, delicious foods spread out before it, garlands of flowers or rupee notes around its neck. These offerings were to accompany the spirit to the Land of the Ancestors, so that when its relatives asked, "What did you bring me?" he or she would have something to give. Other delicacies were burned so the spirit itself could enjoy their essence.

Hundreds of people would come to the *pae*, and the hospitality offered them would bring merit to the deceased, smoothing its path to the afterlife. At night while the priests' chanting continued, guests and villagers would sing and dance, enjoying the liquor, tea, and snacks provided by the household that followed the large meal served in the evening. Those too tired to stay up all night would find a corner in one of the rooms laid out with mats and squeeze into a space among other sleeping bodies, listening to snatches of song and the reverberating beat of the priests' drums. The mourners and their relatives were constantly busy caring for the needs of the guests, though for periods they were pulled from the social world and brought into the ritual. For them it was not a happy time. A father, a brother, a daughter, a wife, someone close had died and now after a time of confusion and pain wandering in the *bardo* between death and rebirth, the person was there with them again. The effigy was its body. Its presence was palpable: the beloved family member had returned for these three days. Mourning women clung to the effigy at twilight when the priests danced, keening stylized mourning chants:

O, my mother, why did you leave me,
O, O, O,
O, my mother take me wherever you go,
O, my mother,
O, O, O.

These would dissolve into sobbing and other women would embrace the grieving relatives, murmuring "Don't cry, don't cry." Their grief was in the center of a crush of spectators around the effigy. Concentric rings: mourners, and the priests who circled them in full regalia, solemn and grand, proclaiming with their presence that the dharma transcends all. Around the outside edges of the crowd, masked jesters played, fielding insults, pinching female bottoms, and prancing away. Grieving men could not weep with abandon, but stood composed, tears trickling down their cheeks. The son would pull the bow on the final evening, shooting an arrow into the twilight sky, the luminous space between day and night, to show the spirit the path to its destination. "They danced intensely and wept intensely," people would say of a successful *pae*. At the end, after the spirit had been released, the bamboo frame, cloth, and bundle of leaves that had been its body would be taken in procession to the edge of the village and dismantled, left like the sky burial of bodies in Tibet, where the corpse was placed out to be dismembered by hungry animals, made an offering to their need.

The shamans wore plain clothes adorned with feathers and bells, rather than the red robes of the lamas. Their ritual was more visceral, a lamb with its throat slit hung over the doorway of a womblike shelter where they did secret work; soul transfer, by which they sent the soul from the effigy to the body of a live sheep through a long slim sliver of bamboo, and the mourners embraced the its woolly body, fed it good food, murmured endearments and pain, breaking into sobs from time to time. Besides the three brothers, there was a shaman from outside Torr who was old and alone, with quiet eyes and a carved bird, who did most of the secret work. I watched and listened with the mountains that hung so huge over Torr, white against the sky even at night, reflecting the moon and the stars. The nearer hills that rolled down from them were dark and looming. The beats of the drums echoed through the gorge.

Pajon told me not to stay up all night. The shamans went into trance and placed their hands in the fire. They chanted a chicken into unconsciousness and hung it upside down over the entrance to the courtyard long after midnight, instructing it to wake when the soul crossed the entryway. After a long stream of chants and gesticulations, it squawked and mourners burst into sobs, calling out to their loved one, disembodied but near.

At rest periods I asked the shamans a question or two and gracious but reserved, they replied, "Never mind, child. Come sit near on our blanket and listen, but never mind these meanings. They are not for you." I let the questions go and sat, sleepy and soft in the dark, the flames of oil lamps flickering close by, listening and watching.

"Not the second night," Pajon said. As Apa's sister, she was in a position of authority. I loved her company and good humor. A tourist had once given us a chocolate bar, passing below the village on her way to Annapurna. I handed it to Pajon: "She said to give it to the children." "Yes," said Pajon, tucking in a stray gray hair and smiling slyly, "little girls like you and me." She broke off two pieces and handed one over.

"Not the second night. Once is enough. If you don't sleep you will get sick."

"But Pajon," I protested, "they are old men and they do not get sick. I am young. I'll be fine."

"They are used to it," she replied, tactfully failing to note that they could command cosmic forces and had other skills and stamina I had not developed.

"Just this once," I pleaded. "The shamans seldom do the *pae*. I may never have another chance."

"All right," she said. The next morning she caught me at the water tap, wet lungi slapping against my cold, clean body. "What are you doing?" she asked. "It's winter." A chill wind blew down from the mountains and the water was icy.

"It's refreshing when you're tired," I said, as I dried my hair. She never let me bathe in Torr again.

Her son Siva taught at the local school and ran an inn where he slept at night, so Pajon was alone at the house higher up in the village. Anna, a cousin who was like a sister to Pajon, had married into an adjoining house in the same lineage and had also been widowed young. She and Pajon shared the same courtyard, her three daughters and son helping with the chores. The households were cheerful and harmonious, but Pajon sometimes found the days long and tedious. She missed the Peace Corps volunteer who had left several months before. He was a sweet and gentle man who had been good company for her. Siva stayed down at the inn, and Pajon's arthritis prevented her going up and down the mountainside easily. I stayed to rest after the *pae*, glad of her good company and the peace of her small household. When she and Anna were napping and the children had gone off, I went down to the inn to talk with Siva and the other teachers. We had snacks together and chatted, looking out over the rough crags of the nearby hills and the open space of the gorge where large birds swooped down and wheeled, their wing feathers spread so the light came through. I thought of the feathered shamans as I sat finishing my tea when the others had gone. Then I felt strange. I could hardly lift my hand to hold the glass. I leaned on the rough boards of the inn's veranda, feeling weak and dizzy. I felt scared to be there alone and stepped little by little up the path, steadying myself against the stone walls that flanked it. When I got to the courtyard, Pajon was out and the children had returned. I went into Anna's house, where she was making tea. "I think I need to lie down," I said, and sank onto the cot.

"Are you sick?" she asked.

"Maybe," I answered. The cool darkness of the house felt so good. I was feeling hot. Anna looked at me with concern. She was plump and kind.

When I had seen her on a trail months after my initial visit to Torr, we had spoken at a resting place and she had laughed and exclaimed half seriously, "Look at you. I thought you were a deaf-mute and now you can talk!" She seemed pleased with her life even though it was hard. I could not drink the tea, and Pajon moved me next door to the cot by her hearth when she got home.

At Pajon's, above where I lay was the altar. She had a scroll painting of a red-robed Buddha hanging there and a butter lamp, an incense brazier where she sprinkled fragrant dried juniper on coals, and a small copper vessel with water. She covered me with a blanket and looked at me with concern as she cooked the evening meal. The flickering of the fire was comforting. So was her presence. My stomach hurt and I could not eat. I alternated between burning heat and chills that shook my body.

"What will you eat?" she asked. This was an unusual question in my experience. Typically in a village people are too busy to pamper the sick. In Tebas, if I did not feel well enough to eat potato curry, Ama dropped by my room to express her regrets and waited for me to show up at the next meal. Sometimes she might bring me a packet of biscuits from the shop. "I could make you some rice pudding," said Pajon. "It is tasty and easy to eat." The idea of swallowing anything brought on waves of nausea. By the next day, Pajon was very worried. "You have to take something, or you will die," she said. "Would you drink lemon water?" Her son had big bottles of lemon concentrate at the inn and it was mixed with sugar and warm water as a drink for tourists. That sounded good.

I am not sure how many days I lay there in that dim room, Pajon leaning over the hearth, stirring glasses of lemon water. Maila came from Tebas to see why I had not returned home after so long, leaving the same afternoon with the news I was unwell. At some point, Pajon moved me to a mat on the floor. I was only vaguely aware of what went on around me, people in and out, some speaking in low serious voices, others poking me in the arm and heartily asking, "Sick!?" I sank deeper into the fever, hot and dry, pushing the blankets off, then reaching for them again when the chills came. I inhabited dreamlike states, hazy spaces between waking and sleep. I felt scared. Pajon looked worried, though she laughed at me when I went outside to relieve myself, tottering and holding on to things, squinting in the light. I seemed to get weaker and sicker each day, till I could hardly get up at all and the bright light of the world seemed quite foreign. Then the blood began to come, running out of my nose without stopping. After the cloths Pajon gave me were full, she brought a shallow basin to catch the flood. As I watched it fill I wondered what foolish thought had brought me to these mountains. Pajon's eyes were rimmed with tears. I should have known when Jane died that it was not good for me to stay. I sank down as Pajon carried the basin away. I looked out the door at the sun on the courtyard and felt angry that I should die so young. I could not drink any more. The heavy blanket smelled like smoke from fire and I huddled into it. I had only a little sense of what went on around me as the day passed. Pajon lit the altar lamp at night and the fragrance of juniper wafted down as the incense drifted past the flame. I slept, and in my dream spirits came and asked for my soul.

"No," I protested, "I cannot. It's not really mine to give." They offered rewards: the ability to change in and out of animal shapes, to become invisible and fly through the air. These were what witches and shamans could do. I refused them.

Perhaps I would like to see the meaning of life, they inquired. I was interested but still refused to give my soul. They said they would show me a little, and as long as I answered only one and not the other when they spoke to me, I could keep my soul. A waterfall of images followed, the most ordinary things: babies, old people, people making love, people who were sick, a girl with an open face. "Oh," I realized after a moment, "it's me."

Though ordinary, all these images were perfect and luminous yet filled with sadness; sweet, like regret for something wonderful that has passed. I could not tell the spirits apart any longer. Afraid, I cried out for them to stop the images. Then I awoke. My body felt soft and cool. The parching fever was gone. It was morning and Pajon had gone out. The house was empty and outside the world was white. The snow that marked the edge of the Himals, always a little bit away, above, had come down and covered the village. One continuous, flowing river of white ran from the peaks to the doorway. I crawled over and looked out the door, feeling the fresh wind on my face. I was kneeling in Annapurna's lap, and I was going to be all right. Pajon came round the house and shouted at me to get out of the cold, then she smiled.

* * *

I could not believe that Mina, so much stronger than I was, could be so sick. My symptoms, too, had matched the description of typhoid, the telltale rose spots appearing on my chest as I recovered, tiny flowers that faded when I got well. I offered to pay to bring her to the hospital in town. Her father stared at the floor and thought, then decided she was not strong enough to make the trip. He knew, too, that those really gravely ill were often refused admittance to the hospital on the principle that the scarce beds should be reserved for people more likely to survive. He summoned a powerful shaman from a nearby village and arranged a soul-calling ceremony.

The ceremony was after dinner on a very dark night. Perhaps there was no moon or maybe the clouds hid its light. The round beam of my flashlight illuminated the jagged flagstones as I walked over, the nearby mountains dark on dark against the sky. I got there early. The shaman was outside with a chicken that would be sacrificed to placate the spirits. The family and a few people were inside the house. Mina continued to babble.

Her eyes were glazed and her hand when I took it was hot and dry, the pulse galloping. Leela came in with her baby and sat next to me, smiling and chatting. I was unsettled by her cheerfulness but tried to be polite. I was unsettled by everything. Mina's babbling was like the chanting of priests come unraveled, a steady stream of words, flotsam and jetsam, this about the millet, that about the buffalo, the world coming undone rather than being knit back together. Priests' chanting creates wholeness out of disorder. Mina was all fragments. Leela nursed her daughter and the room filled up with people till we were sitting knee to knee. The flaming wicks of brass lamps lit the room. The chanting began, not just the shaman, but all of us: "Come back, Mina, come back." Over and over we repeated it and louder and louder it built, ending in a crescendo. Mina stirred then slipped away again. She rested quietly for a while before the babbling continued, low and gentle. I left at that point, glad to be alone in the dark. Ama and Bunti were sitting by the fire shelling corn when I returned. I joined them. Embers glowed through the ashes adding to the soft light of the oil lamp. It felt good to pull the dry kernels off the cob, simple and real.

"She seemed a little better when I left," I said. "I hope she'll be all right." Ama looked at me directly.

"Ernestine," she said, "no one comes back from delirium here."

Mina died at the end of a *pae* for an old man at the top of the village. Tebas was filled with visitors. As I walked down after the final ceremonies had concluded and night had fallen, someone took my arm.

"Mina is going," she said. "Come." We went to her house. People had packed into the room. There were villagers and many strangers. Death always draws a crowd. The neighbor who brought me pushed me forward through the people. Mina lay near the hearth. She was silent. Her eyes were half-closed, dull little slits, and her cheeks were drawn in, lips slightly parted. Rita stood over her.

"O my sister, O my sister," she began to keen and sob, the sobs in rhythm like the chant. Others around me began to weep.

I felt heavy and empty inside, and then it was as though a throbbing took over my body and I began to sob in rhythm with the others, the cries rising out of my body while I held the house pole to stay upright, "O, O, O, Mina, O, O, O, little sister."

Her father stood up. "She is not gone," he said. The mourning stopped. People stifled their cries. "Come rub her feet," he said. For a long time we took turns massaging butter oil into her legs and arms. Her limbs were light and frail and her breath so shallow it was barely there. Finally the neighbor led me out into the night. We crossed the path together, then parted. I continued on through the arched gateway, across our courtyard. The doors to the house were shut. In the house next to my room, young men and women were singing. Sleepless, I joined them. They sang parts separately, the men, then the women, then the men again, on and on, joining together for the refrain that punctuated each part. The parts were improvised, led by a single voice hovering in the stillness with starlight through the open door. It was hypnotic. I relaxed into the lilting voices, appreciating the room made for me in the circle. A single voice soared; the others rose to meet it. Footsteps on the porch: a pause.

"Mina," said the boy in the doorway. "Gone to death."

An intake of breath. The voices completed the refrain.

All night long they sang on Mina's porch. They were her friends. People from the village sat through the night with the family, coming and going in pairs or alone, three or four from a household; sitting for a while and chatting, then returning home. Rita's father made tea and Rita served it. Mina lay where she had died, by the hearth, still wearing her cherry-red blouse.

In the morning they dressed her in finery. A sari, for the most special occasions. When I had first worn one Ama was with her friends and said, "You look so pretty. Now you must dance." They sang and clapped while I stepped and turned in the courtyard, bangles jingling. "Just like in the cinema!" they said approvingly. Mina was very still. She wore red-flecked bangles and above and below those they put thick bracelets, so bright they looked fierce, the savage yellow of pure gold. Her hair was smoothed and braided and a gold headdress shaped like the moon placed above her fore-head, anchored with graceful chains. She looked like a princess in effigy. Her eyes were closed and her skin was dull and rubbery, lips sunken, cheeks gaunt. Her beauty was only a memory, tended and adorned by the women who loved her, as they dressed her to be gazed on for the last time. Her father strapped her to a chair. The village had gathered in the courtyard. Bunti stood with the group who had been Mina's closest friends. We all cried.

"What loss is it to you that you should weep?" snapped one of the girls.

Bunti laid her hand on my arm. "Mina won't come to call her 'elder sister' any more," she said. The girl looked at me. Mina was lifted resplendent in her chair. Her gold ornaments gleamed in the pale morning sun.

Incense was lit. The lama chanted softly then took up his drum. A male relative from the mother's side carried a great white cloth, unfurled like a banner behind him. Mina followed in her chair with the villagers behind her in procession. The drumbeats resounded through the gorge. At other times, we had heard them from other villages and looked out from the courtyard to see the procession, white banner in front and a line of tiny people going down the mountain like ants. "Who has died?" we would wonder. The procession was solemn and quiet, some tears, an occasional murmur: "So young." "So beautiful." "A good girl like that." Rita's aunt supported her as she walked, a shawl covering her face as she cried. After an hour down the steep steps we reached Dusam where Amrit Kumari joined us, shaking her head as tears rolled down her cheeks. It was only a little way from there, softly sloping, to the cremation ground by the river. The rice fields were bare, after harvest and before planting. The river bubbled gently, not yet fed by the melting snows that gave it the force that swept the little winter bridges away. They lay Mina down on the bank. The lama sat and read a small portion of text. "Come away," someone said, and the crowd turned and moved back up the path. They would strip her now and burn her body, sending her into the next life naked as she had come into this one. People lingered together for most of the day, absorbing the death and taking comfort in the huddled company of others, drinking tea, playing cards, braiding each other's hair. We could see the smoke waft up from the river, gray on gray against the clouds that had settled in. I had to be away for Mina's *pae* but I was told that people wept intensely and danced intensely, and that the young ones sang all night without stopping.

4.

The Intimate Darkness
of Shadows and Margins

A few weeks after Mina died, Amrit Kumari was visiting the village in the evening. A soldier home on leave had been drinking and was lurching up the trail as night fell. "Watch out," she said, "Mina's ghost will jump out and grab you." Along the path at the entrance to the village was a stand of bamboo, a clump of tall stalks whose leaves rustled when the air stirred. It was stark, at the edge of the stone path and a bare field where infants were buried and effigies thrown away. Spirits of the restless dead were believed to linger there, waiting to possess vulnerable passersby. Those who had died young or tragically were believed most likely to remain near. Their shock at death or clinging to life prevented them letting go and taking a new birth. They lurked, causing illness or mishap: lonely, greedy, and miserable. Those afflicted by their rage left offerings at the crossroads to assuage the spirits' hunger. "Mina's died?" asked the soldier, newly arrived, and stumbled home to his mother and wife.

The night that Mina had died, I sat with Agai and Tson by the hearth for a while after we had visited her home. We talked for some time, stirring the coals to revive their warmth. I felt bleak and weary and retired for bed. The moon hung in the sky like a wafer as I crossed the courtyard to my room. The image of Mina's corpse lying by the fire would not leave my mind. I thought of going back to the house but was too tired to talk any longer. I bolted the door and window and lay down under the covers. No light penetrated the clay walls. It was so dark I could not see my hands but the room was small and I knew it well, so the darkness posed no hazard. As I lay there, I felt something drop on me. I froze in fright and held my breath. It was the weight and size of something a little larger than a cat, with four paws on my chest and belly. Slowly it walked across my body, each paw pressing into my flesh, and I felt it push off against my knee as it soundlessly jumped down. I listened for its steps in the silent room but heard nothing. I lay still, breathing softly, and waited. My hands trembled as I reached for the flashlight under my bed. Then I turned on the beam and swung myself to a sitting position. I shone the light around. There was nothing there. I looked under the bed: nothing. Corners, the chinks by the ceiling, the small space behind my chest of clothes: nothing. How did it get out? I checked the door and window. Both were bolted from the inside. A hallucination? But it was so palpable. I unbolted the door and ran across the courtyard to the house. Ama had come home and gone to sleep but Tson and Agai still sat by the fire. I told them what had happened. "Death creates a space," said Agai, "where uncanny things can enter."

There used to be regular visits by uncanny things in the village, according to Pajon. Our house, where she grew up, was at the edge, then, against the fields. A branch of the main path through the village ran along behind it. At night the darkness of the village is very pure. If the moon is full, children come out in the courtyards and play and people go visiting after dinner. When the moon is small or in its dark phase, the paths are empty. Occasionally someone will come on a special errand, carrying a flashlight or a flaming torch of long, dry sticks, footsteps punctuating the silence, but that is rare. All the cacophony of the day: children shouting, buffaloes lowing, roosters crowing, people calling out to one another, goats bleating, is stilled. In this still, empty darkness, strange things appear. Pajon told me that headless beings with lamps on their shoulders used to dance behind their house in the deep night, tall and stately, flames glowing as they moved and swayed. Sometimes one would come on a horse, stand for a moment and then go on. "They were only seen rarely," she said, "but now they do not come at all." "Why?" I asked. She did not know.

Returning from Torr by way of Cliff Shelter, I asked Bhimsen why they no longer came. He agreed that fewer otherworldly beings visited the region in recent times. "I think they need wilderness to flourish," he said, "and there is less of that. Perhaps they also need to be believed in. Fewer people do now. Some say such things are nonsense. The wild forest is going and people are skeptical. Perhaps this place no longer seems hospitable to them."

The river played behind us and a cool wind blew down from the mountains as we talked. Trekkers walked by with their backpacks and slouchy striding pace. I looked out at prayer flags flapping near the river. Maila lama, a respected priest from the north, was doing a purification ritual in a tall house by the riverbank and the soft sound of distant drumbeats drifted down to us. A mule train approached the wooden plank bridge suspended over the fierce frothing water where it met the shallower river I had walked along. Manju, Bhimsen's daughter, a little younger than me, came to sit with us. The mules clopped past with their headdresses bobbing. The mule driver called out to Bhimsen in Tibetan and he replied. The light grew dim as the winter evening fell, and someone rang the bell at the little temple, ding-ding, sharp against the deeper rush of the water. The river seemed to grow louder at night when other sounds had stopped. Bhimsen went in, and Manju and I sat quietly as the mountain cast its shadow over the small stone street.

*　*　*

In late winter there are no festivals, because it is believed that in the month of Magh that overlaps January and February, the deities all go to bathe in sacred rivers. The hillsides are rocky and bare, the landscape like a pen and ink drawing, a Chinese painting come to life. The rhythm of the village slows and draws inward; the land rests and people create and bring in what the village will need when the fields demand their attention again. Women sit in their courtyards with looms in their laps weaving carrying cloths, rain covers, shawls. Men thread strips of bamboo back and forth in diamond patterns to make baskets. "People are jealous because mine are the best," Apa said playfully. Young men and women carry last year's baskets to the forest, bringing their axes, and return to build the woodpiles higher. They joke and flirt as they head down the path. Boys and girls with little scythes go to cut fodder for the animals. Those from wealthier households sit in rows in the schoolhouse, reciting in unison the lesson the teacher has given, then pouring out and running down the path at the end of the day, bookbags bumping behind them. Dinner is eaten close in by the fire, the coals stirred for their warmth for a long time after. No one would be so profligate as to burn the scarce wood for comfort. The sun in the courtyard and an extra shawl shield against the cold. On really bitter days, the old ones stay in bed huddled under thick cotton quilts.

After Mahg is the month of Phalgun, February/March, when the weather turns warm again. On the Phalgun full moon, there is a celebration. It is a tradition of the Thakali people from the north, and initially the Thakali families in the region participated, young ones singing and dancing and adults chatting, drinking, and playing cards through the night. Since it took place on the wide flat fields below the village, local Gurungs joined the festivities and it became a huge event, all the more convivial for the crowds. I went with Ama one year on a balmy night. The moon washed the fields white and we needed the flashlight only through the jungle. I padded behind her on the path, contentedly watching the circle of light bobbing ahead. The wide terraces with dry rice stubble were filled with people, and besides the usual tea shop that was set up for the winter with clay walls and a thatched roof, there were a couple of lean-tos where warm liquor, tea, and snacks were being served. People clumped around these and milled about on the rice terraces.

A stage was set up and young men danced as girls and boys sang together out of sight, a drum punctuating their singing. They sang fashionable songs from the radio, not the hypnotic music of the village. One of the boys on the stage wore women's clothes and swayed his hips as the male figure mimed the song and leaned toward him. Grown women could not dance before men. The words drifted down, "Pretty young girl . . ." The Magar woman who had married Rita's father's brother sat in a circle of men, sleek and laughing, and her husband stood to one side drinking and watching her. Others cast glances in her direction as she tossed her head back, veil slipping down her shoulder.

I had a feeling of vertigo surrounded by all the people. Many strangers from other villages had come. Some were drunk. Occasionally a glance would be followed by a double-take and a flashlight would shine in my face. Ama had disappeared with her friends. I could see no one I knew. A man brushed by me and leered. A group of teenage girls approached laughing and took hold of my sleeve and my shawl, fingering my bangles and touching my hair, talking about me without addressing me at all. When I spoke to them, they laughed again, "She can talk!" and then moved on. I felt scared in the midst of all the swirling people and hurried from group to group searching for Ama. I could not find her anywhere. I ran into a neighbor from the village.

"Have you seen my mother?"

"No," he replied, "but she is sure to be around here somewhere."

"Hey, white-woman," shouted a group of passing boys.

I continued to look, feeling a growing sense of disorientation and fear; unanchored in the crowd, looking for this mother whose presence would bring me relief. She defined me in that world and now I was floating and strange, feeling my strangeness too intensely. I looked up the hillside at the forest. It was dark and still. A stream spilled out of it above the path. Nearer the forest the crowds thinned out. I headed that way. I needed quiet and space. People glanced at me as I walked away from the activity, spinning off from the center that drew the others. As I moved closer to the trees I could hear the water gurgling. The trees threw shadows across the moonlit ground. I did not hesitate but plunged into the dark. I was alone. Voices drifted up from the fields, incomprehensible in the distance. A tinkle of laughter. The forest was very dark but my feet knew the path. The dark felt ominous and I walked quickly. It felt good to be quick and purposeful. I broke through on the fields below our house. The doors were bolted but I opened my room and lay down without lighting a lamp, soothed by the dark and the silence. I felt my breathing and the quiet for a long time. The buffalo rustled in the stable. I had meant to stay there, but after a while I felt lonely. Ama might wonder where I was. The moonlight was so pretty. Maybe Leela would be there. I stood up, smoothed my hair and shook out my lungi. Returning to the forest, it seemed more forbidding now I was not fleeing from anything. I stood on the edge and looked, then walked quickly into the trees, down the slope, along the stream, straight along the mountainside, then was disgorged into the moonlight and rice stubble.

As I entered the crowd I spotted Ama. She saw me cross the fields.

"Where did you go?" she asked.

"There were so many people," I said, "and I couldn't find you. I got scared and went home for a while."

"Alone through the jungle in the dark?" she asked.

"Yes," I replied.

"There is a lot more to be afraid of there than here," she said. "Come."

I sat with her and her two friends Amre and Ammaili. They joked and commented on the passersby. Then we went to a tea stall and had some snacks. I drifted through the crowd with them, listening to small groups of people sing, watching some card games, conversing here and there. People greeted us. I recognized faces in the crowd now. It did not seem such a frightening, unknown mass. I wondered that I should have panicked so. I felt sleepy but safe and content with these women. The night had nearly passed, though the mountains across the gorge were still dark shadows against the moonlit sky. We settled down on a terrace near the stage and watched a young Thakali girl dance, braid swinging as she stepped forward and back, her hands rising gently with the movement, wrists turning delicately. The great white moon began to set behind her, slipping behind the mountain little by little, eaten by the night. As the last beam of light was extinguished there was a moment of darkness, then, in a breath, the first ray of sunlight shot from the ridge behind us and hit the hill that had swallowed the moon. A bird sang. The girl danced, people stirred themselves and as the day dawned they moved in the different directions of home.

*　　*　　*

Activity started slowly in the spring. When it was still cold, the potatoes were planted. These went in the fields higher on the mountainside. Tebas was famous for its delicious potatoes and farmers walked from villages two days away with their battered baskets to trade for seed potatoes in the early spring. As the weather warmed and big blue butterflies played in the meadows near Cliff Shelter, it was time to plant corn. This went in the fields nearer the village. The land was rocky and the fields needed to be cleared of stones and the ground broken after winter. Sometimes I helped, swinging the short-handled hoe over my head and chopping the earth till it yielded soft crumbled soil. Ama would stop me after a while. "You are not accustomed to this work. Go now and rest." The oxen would finish what we had started, hauling the wooden plow across the small terraces, down to the end, turning tightly, back again, until the field was marked with neat rows, ready to receive the seeds.

As the little corn plants were growing with their crisp leaves, thunderstorms came down from the north. The thunder echoed in the gorges and in Torr where the mountains around the village were higher, the thunder and rain would grow faint and soft and then would return again, bounced off the opposite ridge. The storms would spend themselves careening back and forth between the ridges, the thunder drifting off and returning again, rain pounding the slate roofs and courtyards, easing for a while and then coming back. The streams that had dried so that women stood for a long time to fill their water jugs with a thin trickle began to swell and gush again. The harsh mountainsides softened with green. There was more coming and going from the village to the fields, but the planting season had not reached its summer pitch of intensity. There was time to visit still and though the rivers began to grow large, they had not yet gained the force to wash the winter bridges away or make the shallows impossible to ford. In the summer, people are bound to home. The land demands their labor and the rivers rise up and hem them in, so that the only paths that are open are high, slippery, and dangerous. The bells of the mule trains stop and the priests from the north return to their homes, temperate above the monsoon.

Before the rivers rose again, I went to see Pajon. Visiting her was so simple. Only the family around the courtyard, not throngs of villagers, peddlers and passersby. Everyone came to the headman's house in Tebas. I had thought initially that Jimwal ("headman") was Apa's name and wondered why our house was the center of such unrelenting activity. "No," said Gopal, Badhay's son and so a brother-by-adoption to me. (The children of brothers or of sisters were considered siblings, drawing the net of relationship close.) He laughed, showing the square white teeth in his round handsome face, eyes curving up a bit, like Ama's. "Jimwal means the leader. In the old days, he was like the king of the village. He is still like that. He offers hospitality and solves problems, gives advice and organizes work, like clearing paths and building the school. Of course everyone comes here. Village meetings and rituals are held here, too."

By comparison, Pajon's house was lonely, high on the side of the mountain, in a nook off the path, just her, Anna, and their children around the courtyard. Pajon's joints were swollen with arthritis but she still managed the household. Her son, Siva was small, nervous but kind, with a serious face. His gaze was direct when he spoke. He generally stayed down at the inn he had opened on the trekking path above the school, rather than in his mother's house near the top of the village, but I often saw him when I visited. I liked his thoughtful manner, and enjoyed his quiet company. After school, he usually sat on the veranda of his inn with the other teachers looking out over the gorge and the mountains, and I joined them sometimes. He had gone to college in Pokhara and had returned to Torr to teach at the high school. There was some tension between him and his mother. When it came time to arrange his marriage, he had agreed that his mother should choose the bride, but insisted on having an educated girl. His mother had chosen the elder of two sisters in Sohrya, a nearby village. He had been happy with this choice, as she was one of the most educated girls in the area and had a pleasing personality. His mother had proceeded on the way to make the betrothal when she had encountered a friend on the path. Explaining her errand, they talked, and the friend expressed serious misgivings. As a widow with an only son, Pajon would be entirely dependent on this daughter-in-law. Didn't she know about educated girls? They did not want to stay at home and do the bidding of the mother-in-law. Educated girls were strong-minded and defiant. She would probably want to go and live in the city. Her friend suggested she was making a grave mistake to bring this girl into her home. With her own misgivings, Pajon was shaken. After all, this educated son looked at the local deity and said it was only a stone. He was respectful, but then he was her own son. Who could tell with a bride? "The younger sister is not educated," said the friend, "and she is very docile and sweet. Ask for her." So Pajon did, and in order not to humiliate his mother, the girl, and himself, Siva went through with the marriage. The elder sister married someone else and proved an excellent daughter-in-law. Siva refused to live with his new wife and stayed down at the inn alone, and his bride remained in Sohrya with her family. Pajon was contrite and very lonely. She liked my visits and I enjoyed the intimacy and freedom of her quiet house and empty courtyard. When she was well enough, we spent the afternoons down at the inn, and came up at nightfall for dinner and long conversations as the fire burned down.

One evening, she settled herself by the fire after our meal, and told me of the strange twists her fate had taken, leaving her there in the house by the mountains alone. She had grown up in Tebas, the headman's youngest daughter. The village was smaller. There had been more livestock, great herds of goats and buffaloes brought up to the high pastures above the jungle in summer by her brothers and the servant boys. The forest was near, larger and darker, less wood cut for use and cleared for farming. The trees came nearly to the house, and getting firewood meant stepping out and chopping few branches, not the long treks that I had been on with Tson and Saras where we had to search carefully for dead wood.

World War I came and her father went to fight and returned with a pension. Now they had cash to supplement his ample land and the family gold. "Subedar," his military rank, was added to his hereditary titles. He loaned money and it grew. He sponsored dance-dramas and feasts, adding honor to the house. Their home was the hub of the village; supplicants for aid and advice, traveling holy men and merchants, the important men of the village all came around. Children and passersby stopped in to see what excitement there might be in their courtyard. Sacrifices and dances enacting the life of Krishna were performed before their veranda, with all the village crowded around. Their family enjoyed wide respect. Her father was a kind man, and if a loan could not be repaid, he forgave it, securing a permanent debt of gratitude and obligation. His influence was wide. Pajon's elder brothers married. Atay came as the first bride, the daughter of an army friend of Pajon's father, another village aristocrat. Then Lalita was brought, beautiful and slim, from Torr. Ama's lineage was old and pure, descendents of those who were the kings of Torr at the height of its greatness, and her father, more ruthless in business than the Subedar, was very wealthy. She and Pajon were close in age and became inseparable. Pajon had an elder sister but lost her at an early age. Just into her teen years, the sister felt stomach pains one day and was dead by evening. "Just like that," Pajon said. At nine, Pajon was given in marriage to the house in which she now lived.

She had been a bright and lively child, with black, black hair and large round eyes. Her parents indulged her. The house was full of servants. In those days, debt or certain legal offenses could cause one to be enslaved and several slaves lived in their household. ("We don't talk about that now, or say who was enslaved," Pajon told me. "It isn't nice.") The children did a little work if it pleased them or if their mother needed special help, but Pajon generally spent the day playing around the village with friends. Marriage was a shock. It meant obediently carrying out the commands of her mother-in-law, never expressing wishes or discomfort, being quiet and demure in the presence of others. Her honor and that of her family depended on her good behavior. Compared to the house she was raised in, grand and in the center of everything, the one she came to was dark, dull, and tucked away in a corner. Tebas faces west and a little south and is sheltered from the cold Himalayan winds. Torr is not. The clouds come down from the mountains and the wind is sharp and icy. Torr is spectacular, steep and brutal. Tebas is more soft, verdant, gentle. I thought of how I had come to her house in Torr, new to the hills with my Peace Corps friend, William. "Go to Tebas," she had said. "It is warmer there, and the people are rough but open and kind."

After a month or two in the married household, she would get to return to her home in Tebas for a period of comfort and delicious freedom, but then the day would come when a man would appear at the door, sent by her husband's family, to escort her back to Torr. "I hated to go," she said. "I cried. I was always hungry. In Tebas there was the custom of a midmorning snack, but not in Torr. I felt famished in the daytime and used to go behind the house and cry." Her husband, a teenage boy, brought her treats from time to time. He seems to have been a decent person, but she never discussed him and her only comment about their relationship was that she thought arranged marriage was a bad idea. After a while the pain of the transition faded and the rhythm of her new life became familiar. When visiting Tebas, she and Lalita would wrap their shawls and go to hear the village boys and girls sing back and forth on cool nights by lamplight, sitting on the edge as proper married ones, their girlhoods transformed.

*   *   *

Pajon stirred the coals and they glowed in the darkness, illumining her face. The wick of the lamp had burned low and the room was shadowy.

She shifted her weight on the mat and pulled her shawl more tightly around her, her knuckles swollen. The night was cool. Some hair slipped out of her braid and she pushed it back.

*   *   *

As time went on in her married life, she had three sons, sturdy little boys. Then when Siva was still an infant, her children fell ill. As she tended them, her husband also caught the sickness. They lay on cots and little bedrolls on the floor. The baby recovered first. Day by day the others got worse. Pajon cooked soothing foods for them and boiled healing herbs. She wiped their damp, hot faces with cool cloths. She offered incense and flowers at the altar, and called the lama to make amulets. There was no hospital in the town then, no doctors in the region. Exhausted, she slept fitfully.

Before the boys fell ill, she had dreamed of the village goddess of Tebas. Waking one morning, as she nursed little Siva, she recalled having had that dream. Her voice was soft and sad when she told me, "I dreamt of the goddess and did nothing. I sent no offering. I made no sacrifice. Now my family was dying. Sakti was punishing me." The goddess Sakti lived in a shrine in the forest above Tebas. I had never been there. Women and pigs, considered impure, were not allowed near the area. Sakti was fierce, wild, and ruthless. People from other villages came at times of crisis or need to plead for her help. To be in her favor was to be greatly blessed. If slighted or offended, she was unsparing. Some people of the untouchable castes had lived below her shrine until one of their hogs had run on its piggy legs into the grass surrounding it. Enraged, she cast a landslide down on their hamlet and destroyed it, killing several people. They rebuilt further away. Pajon was shaken to think she had neglected the goddess. She sent a young goat to be sacrificed. Its throat was cut with a large curved knife and blood sprayed on the altar. "But," she told me, "it was too late. The goddess was angry. My big boys died and my husband. I was left alone with little Siva, scared I might lose him, too." Widowed in her early twenties, her sole security this fragile infant, she felt sad and alone. The mountain gorge was steep and harsh and cold winds blew down from the icy Himals all winter. Her husband was an only son and his parents had died, so there was no one at home in Torr to guide and console her, to comfort her grief and soothe her guilt. She clung to the baby and nurtured him. Her father came. Two brothers had been killed in World War II and her mother had died of grief. Her father sat with her and held her hand.

In spring before the heavy monsoon rains, when the quiet, dry earth was coming back to life the year that her boys had died, Pajon's father took her on pilgrimage. Five days' walk north of the village, on the far side of the Himals where the Tibetan plateau sweeps into Nepal, there is a temple complex called Muktinath, "Place of Liberation." It is one of the most sacred shrines in South Asia, holy to both Hindus and Buddhists. I went there, too, more than thirty years later, and often pictured Pajon young and sad, walking over the hills and past the mountains to the temple. When it was still closed to foreigners friends from the village had gone, bustling and lively like Chaucer's pilgrims, and returned to tell of their adventures and the joy of receiving blessings from such a holy place.

There are two possible paths north. Pajon and her father could have gone up through the river gorge from Tebas, climbing the near-vertical steps to Melori, but they chose the more direct trail from Torr. That path is easier and shorter, but dangerous for going through the thick, dark rainforest that covers the mountain above the villages. At the beginning it is clear and open, facing the cold wall of the Annapurnas as it snakes along the side of the mountain away from the village. Without the sheltering walls of houses the wind comes down in full force. Suddenly the landscape seems bare and feels exposed, raw and frightening. The high, wild ridges ripple toward the north and the white Annapurnas are unfurled against the sky, subtle and harsh. Here the path enters the jungle, the rainforest so dense a guide is needed to get through it, otherwise, as villagers said to me, "People get lost and die there." This had happened. In spring the tiger lilies push up through the sod and orchids climb languidly up the trunks of trees. It is silent and misty; moss and shadows. The path, obscure at best, is hidden further by fallen rhododendron blossoms that turn the forest floor red and crush underfoot like Chinese silk. Shafts of sunlight penetrate here and there. There are rumors of leopards and small black bears, sleek and snuffling, hidden in the mist.

After a day's walk, the forest path reaches the main trail again. It is like coming out of a movie theater in the afternoon, moving into a new reality, brighter and more defined. There are the inns, verandas occupied by resting travelers, chatting in the light, the clink and rattle of brass dishes being set down on rough wooden tables. Tibetan and Thakali traders and those who set up temporary inns on unused winter rice fields, lamas who come down to offer rituals for Buddhist lowlanders, like those in Cliff Shelter, the usual mule drivers, a few pilgrims all head north when the weather becomes warmer. After a long day of walking, an inn is a welcome sight. People sit in clumps, eating and chatting, having warm rice liquor or a cup of tea after dinner, watching night fall as little lamps are lit by the innkeeper's wife or daughters. After it is dark some linger on but most go up to the long attic room where rows of cots are laid out with cotton mattresses, pillows, and quilts, fragrant with wood smoke from the fire below. Some conversation continues in the dark, and then people sleep until the soft light of dawn filters through the eaves and each group stirs and repacks their bundles, ready to move on.

As the main path goes north, it meets thick fir forests lining a gorge that becomes steeper and narrower as it continues. The path creeps along the side of it. This is the path that slips between two great mountains, where the Annapurna range meets Dhaulagiri Himal. Beyond the pass the land opens out. There are villages of stone houses with low flat roofs, like mosaics from above, the tiles decorated with sheaves of grain spread to dry in the sun. There are steppe-like hills with high grass flattened by the wind where men, red ribbons woven through the braids wrapped around their heads, graze their sheep. The wind catches fragments of the high haunting songs they sing to pass the time. The wind is constant, rising in the early afternoon and blowing until nightfall.

It was something of a foreign land to Pajon and her father. Tibetan rather than Nepali was the common language there. The Dalai Lama still ruled further north in Lhasa and the area just below Muktinath was an important trading center, clan chiefs vying for control of the salt trade across the open border with Tibet. At that time Maila lama studied with the teacher he venerated in one of the great monasteries in the Tibetan capital. The closing of the border by the Chinese invaders ended the salt trade and the lively, prosperous trading villages became like ghost towns as the merchants who inhabited them moved south to start other ventures (like the inns of Cliff Shelter). Maila lama's teacher was killed by the soldiers and his monastery ravaged and closed and the lama became part of the long trail of refugees walking over the barren wastes toward Nepal. His family received him, thin and tired and full of grief to have seen the sacred world that had been his home for thirty-five years gouged and chopped, walls broken, shrines desecrated, monks and nuns lying dead and bloody in the courtyards as more and more Chinese convoys entered the city. In Nepal he trekked down to the lowlands with his assistants during the cold winters, back to his home in Dorje for the pleasant summers, performing rituals to purify and bestow blessings on households in the villages, remembering perhaps the great monastic ceremonies of Lhasa as he sat in the dimly lit attics of village homes. His religion lay light but deep in him. He was funny and warm, and so sincere, said one client, that he could hardly get a joke. He was always friendly and welcoming when I came, sometimes with local women, sometimes alone, to hear the drums and bells and chants, and the beautiful wailing long-horns of their rituals.

Pajon and her father stayed the night in Dorje, since Maila lama's aunt was a ritual-friend to Lalita, which meant that each of them took on the obligations of family to one another, using kin terms and both offering and expecting hospitality, just as family members would. Maila lama's family, wealthy enough to spare a son for the monastery and send him to be educated in Lhasa, had a large house with an enclosed courtyard, low, not tall like Gurung houses, with the rooms built around and sheltering the inner court.

The path to Muktinath continues north, past the nearly underground village of Kagbeni, built low against the driving wind, and the high citadel town of Jarkot, an ancient walled kingdom. Beyond that there are open hills and grasslands, and a last inn where pilgrims to the shrine can spend the night. It is high and cold there. In April snow still lies on the ground. Approaching the temple complex, the land is barren and wild. Inside there is a wall with 108 stone serpent heads spouting water, plentiful in spring when the snow on the lower flanks of the Himals has begun to melt. The line of snakes emerging from the stone, gushing stream upon stream of cascading water, are regal and forbidding. Their water, clear and cold, is believed to purify sins, cleansing all defilements so that any obstacles to spiritual freedom and wholeness are removed. Pajon had walked slowly under each one, she said, in the chill air of the temple courtyard, drenching herself with absolution.

*   *   *

Like Pajon and her father, I stayed in Dorje at Maila lama's house when I, too, went to Muktinath in spring. His mother had died and he, whom I had walked so far to see, had just entered a two-month period of isolated meditation, cloistered in a shrine room filled with beautiful and terrifying Buddhist images, meals and notes slipped in but no other contact with the world. He received my note and gift. On the morning I was to leave, he sent a note expressing sorrow at missing me and instructing his kind sister to give me a carpet his mother had woven. When I walked out past the high stone pillars and prayer flags that marked the entrance to Dorje, carrying the golden wool carpet on my back, I cried, wondering when I would see him again.

Going on to Muktinath, I walked alone from Dorje. The beginning was easy. The path sloped up gradually and meandered along near the river in places. I had never seen anything like the vast openness of the place. The empty land reached up, soft sloping browns and grays, into the empty sky, and the wind blew relentlessly. The path became steep after a while, going higher and higher above the river, until it looked like a silver line beneath me. The mountainside was shale and there was a clear drop to the river below. I looked ahead, not down, or attended to my footsteps on the path ahead, little flat shale pieces glinting on the ground. Halfway along the mountainside there had been a landslide and the path was wiped out for about fifty yards. There were some footprints across the gash but I was not brave enough to try it. I turned back and returned to the river. Someone pointed out another path and I went ahead, reaching Kagbeni. It was a strange village whose twisted streets seemed to be built mainly underground, as they were covered against the wind. I had Tibetan tea from innkeepers there who stared at me but spoke very little. Then I went on to Jarkot, wild and forbidding with its towering walls and tight-packed houses. I walked a long time on its narrow streets trying to find my way through to the other side, then finally reached the open land again. By that time the wind had been blowing for hours and I wrapped a shawl across my face against the dust.

Beyond Jarkot, I took the wrong path and wandered through the open wastes, light-headed from the altitude. My small bag felt heavy and I was gasping from the thin air. The sun began to set and the landscape seemed eerie. I looked around and wondered which way to go. As I stood on a hillock and stared out at the sweeping hillsides and rising land, a nun with short gray hair and a round face approached me, her red robes flapping in the wind. "Do you know the way to Muktinath?" I asked. "Come with me," she said. "I am going there. There is no place for travelers at the temple, but I will bring you to the inn where pilgrims stay." Relieved, I fell into step with her. She reached for my bag. "I'll carry this," she said. I protested that it was more proper that I should carry her things but she insisted, saying I was obviously unused to walking up so high, and firmly took the bag away. Her help made it much easier to go on, though I felt ashamed to be loping along next to her while she, an old woman, shouldered my burdens. We walked quietly together until we came to a plain square building, the inn. "Stay here," she said, "and come to the temple in the morning." Then she turned away and went on.

I slept with all my clothes and my jacket on, still shivering. It was so much colder than it had been below, even in Dorje. In the morning I went to the temple, an easy hour's walk from the inn. It was small and modest, unlike the high, many-roofed golden temples of Kathmandu, and had a single roof tapering to delicate curved points at each corner and a small embossed golden door. I walked by the serpent fountains gingerly splashing the ice-cold holy water on my forehead, remembering Tson's instruction that in cold weather just a little holy water purifies very nicely, but feeling chagrined when I thought of Pajon bravely drenching herself so many years before under those streams, the water soaking her hair, her clothes wet and dripping. I felt cowardly as I dipped my fingers in just a little, but was deeply pleased to be there at all. In the past, the area north of Dorje had been closed to foreigners, and I had often heard of Muktinath and wished that I could go, always imagining it permanently out of reach, a holy land forbidden to me.

As I stood there in the mist that came off the streaming water, contentedly looking about, the nun from the evening before appeared and greeted me. "Come and make your devotions," she said, "and then we'll have tea." I blinked in surprise. "I live here," she said, "and care for the temple. The Brahmin priests are here in the warm season, but through the winter, we Buddhist nuns look after the temple." I followed her.

Knowing the most sacred Hindu shrines are open only to devotees, I thought I would just stand outside the shrine and pay my respects. I remembered the time in Kathmandu when as I walked near the slow, curving Bagmati river I accidently got too close to the wall of the great temple at Pasupatinath and was shooed away by irate worshippers. A dog with a torn ear had sat with his back against the wall gnawing something and red-bottomed monkeys clambered along the top of it but I was not allowed near. I sat on the hillside opposite holding back tears. Still, I wanted to make the pilgrimage to Muktinath even though I knew I would not be allowed to go into the sanctum to be received by the deity. I was happy just to approach it.

The nun led me to the temple and took out her key and opened the door. I gazed in, moved and wondering. There it was. I could see the edge of a golden image and the altar surrounding it.

"Go on," said the nun. I looked at her, confused.

"I thought white-people weren't allowed in," I said.

"You have come to do devotions," she replied. "Go and make your offerings." I felt a sweet sense of shock. I stepped across the threshold, a little afraid, and looked at the gentle, half-smiling face of the deity. I stood a long time in the quiet of the small golden room, looking, then I set the offerings on the altar, feeling as though nothing existed but that place and the moment I had been given as an unexpected gift.

She gave me a golden ribbon from the altar and locked the door when I came out. Then the nun led me to her room where we had tea. It was little and dark. I noticed now, too, that her robes were worn. "I have no butter, just oil for the tea," she said. It tasted strange. I had left only a little money in the offering, not wanting to be ostentatious, and now I felt sorry. When I finished the tea, she rose and took me to see an old abandoned Buddhist chapel covered with faded frescoes. It was dark and dusty, with some loose boards in the corner, the red paint on the frescoes crumbling in places. Then she brought me across to the famous Buddhist shrine with the sacred flame that floated on water. It was a large open room, plain except for the Buddha images. I watched the flame burning steadily. It was said to have burned there from the beginning of time.

"Is there oil in the water?" I asked, wondering how this could be. The stream surfaced at an open space on the floor, then went under the shrine and flowed out.

"No," said the nun, "it's pure, just the water and the flame. It burns because the place is so holy. Come, you can drink the water as it flows out." We went around to where the stream flowed out and I knelt down and scooped some up in my hand and drank it. It was pure, cold water. The sky was very blue. I bowed low to the nun, looking at her lined face and soft brown eyes, then stood quietly, my palms still pressed together.

"Go well," she said.

"Stay well," I replied.

I paused once more then turned and stepped back the way I had come, just as the wind was beginning to rise.

I walked down through Dorje, through the pass where the Black Gandaki river cuts between the high mountains, through the pine forest, and under the rhododendron canopy. It was five days of hard walking from there to Tebas. This was the spring not of my first visit to Nepal but a later one. There were water taps in the village now: no more early morning trips to the stream, lines of girls with their curving copper jugs. There was a new school, built on some of the nearby millet fields. Besides these changes, the village looked much the same, clusters of houses, the winding paths, some meeting the main path through the center, some ending in courtyards or going to fields.

Most of the family had gone out to attend to the planting, but I stayed back. Pajon had sent word that she was coming. Filled with warm anticipation, I waited in the quiet courtyard. It had been three years since we had met. I saw her as she stepped through the arched gate. By her side walked a five year old girl with eyes like hers, a sturdy body, and straight black hair. It was Siva's daughter. He had reconciled himself to his marriage and brought his wife to live with him at the inn. Now Pajon stayed there, too. She took off her bag and settled down on the mat. Her face was tired but relaxed and happy. I asked how she had been. "I feel much better these days," she said. "It was hard for many years, but life is good now." Manita, her granddaughter, tugged at her skirt. "She cried so much on the walk," said Pajon, "that I had to give her a rupee to keep her going." "Now give it back," she said to Manita. "It was just to cheer you up." Manita handed her the money and put her head in Pajon's lap. "Children are a lot of work," she said, "but they make life bright." We sat in the sun and looked at the growing corn, talking while Manita rested.

*　　*　　*

So many influences come to bring good fortune and ill, according to village friends. There is one's own destiny, shaped by karma. Then there are the planetary influences, read through astrology. The gods, too, intervene: the great gods of the myths and legends, like Siva and Ram; the local deities, whose influence, being near, is often most powerful. People murmur a prayer: "Sakti of Tebas, earth-god of the hillside, ancestor-deities, our forefather-gods, keep and protect us." These form a triad, guarding three points at the edges of the village, encircling the land and shaping human fates: this village a vortex of destiny, as is any village, any life. The past, present and future converge in each moment, the force of karmic momentum, the pull of this planet or that, a god displeased or well-disposed molding circumstance, and the person responding, groping, like the newborn baby roots for the breast, driven by inner hungers. Each action evokes a response from life, and divination, oracles, dreams illuminate and guide. The restless dead, the angry witch, the uncanny creature from the forest can intervene to cause harm. Ancestors, bodhi-sattvas, shamans can offer protection. The wandering holy man begging for food may be a god. The woman requesting an item one wants not to give may be a witch. A simple act or omission may have unimagined consequences. Pajon woke up and wondered at having dreamt of the village goddess. She did not make an offering. Siva saw that this rejected bride was his fated wife and brought her home. Pajon rested her tired bones on the mat. She lay down and covered her face with her shawl, against the flies and light, and shifted Manita next to her, heavy with sleep. A cock across the village crowed, and I lay down too, and rested with them.

Maili, my middle sister, had a beautiful son. Her daughter, Sumitra, was the eldest, serious and like a perfect small copy of Ama in face and form. I met them only on this very trip when the family had returned from Hong Kong. I liked Sumitra's childish dignity. Ananda, the boy, was lively and bright, with a halo of dark brown hair and wide eyes. He often sat with Apa when he was weaving baskets in the courtyard, watching as the heap of bamboo strips took form, building from a small base to an open mouth big enough for a water jug to rest inside, finally wrapped round at the top so the edge was smooth and the shape firm.

When I last saw Maili, five years after that first meeting, Sumitra was tall and slim, in her early teens, and she had another young son, about seven. Ananda had died. His father told me he had had leukemia. He said the first doctor who had treated him had been very conscientious and Ananda had improved. The doctors who took over the case on the first one's retirement had been careless though, he said, not keeping track of the charts and the proper medication. "They did not care," Man Bahadur said, "because to them we were only Gurkhas, and Ananda worsened and died." He stared at the ground. "He was at the top of his class," he said sadly. "Only eleven years old. We have his soccer trophy." "We spoil the little one," said Maili. "I cannot bear to see him sad since his brother died."

Later when we were alone in the house, Maili took me aside. "It wasn't the doctors," she said. "They did as much as could be done. We took him to a civilian hospital and they confirmed the diagnosis and said the medicine was correct. It wasn't the doctors. I'll tell you what happened. After he had become very sick, we brought him to the shaman. You know, in the military there are some shamans, too, from the villages. He read his pulse and told us that Ananda had been afflicted by a witch, one from our own village, and that her hold was too deep for him to loosen it. He said Ananda could not be helped. Then I remembered. After we saw you, we came again for another trip home. I had some very nice cloth that I had brought from Hong Kong. A woman in the village asked if she could buy it and offered me a sum. It was so little that it hardly covered what I had paid. 'I would rather give it to you,' I told my mother-in-law, 'than sell it to her for so little.' 'Think carefully before you refuse her,' my mother-in-law told me. 'She is known to be a witch.' I thought about it but because my spirit is strong I cannot be harmed by witch attack so I refused. My strength deflected her curse, but it fell on my son. That is why he died. The doctors truly tried to help him." She rinsed the kettle and filled it with water, then poured tea into the china cups and saucers she had brought from Hong Kong.

If the witch has not achieved a hold too deep, a shaman can dislodge the affliction. The most powerful exorcist in the village was a frail old untouchable man, thin, with skin so dark it seemed nearly black. Intense but genial he was called Katwale, "town crier." He made announcements about work parties and celebrations at the headman's request, at junctures where paths met throughout the village. He also acted as leader of the untouchable community attached to the village. The headman's children all addressed him respectfully as Grandfather Katwale and the elders also treated him with courtesy. Gurungs consider graciousness to be a mark of honor and to treat someone else with disrespect is to call your own standing into question. Katwale's natural dignity commanded respect. So did his skill. He was well-known in the area as a powerful shaman. While priests have the power to summon the aid of benevolent forces, the shamans struggle with the forces of darkness. The Gurung shamans were known, too, as spirit guides for souls in the afterlife, but the profiency of the untouchable shamans was with evil spirits, witches, and unknown or unnamable malevolent powers that lurked at the edges of human life.

The untouchables, too, lived at the edge, their hamlet situated between the Gurung village and the forest, the boundary marked by a small stream that tumbled down the mountain. Katwale and his clan were metalworkers, as are many untouchable shamans, shaping iron from the earth with fire, the metal deep red in their tongs, or working pure yellow gold into the scalloped bracelets that Gurung women wore. I met him first when he was called to blow spells into Tson's sick baby. Ratna had been cranky and refusing milk. Katwale knelt while Tson held the baby, closed his eyes tight and mumbled strings of words, then blew at the baby's stomach, three sharp puffs while the baby looked on with serious eyes. He repeated this several times, then brought an offering of bits of food on a small leaf-plate and left it at the crossroads to placate the offending spirit or witch.

They are believed to be always hungry, often bitter and excluded, those who cause pain. People who have died young and tragically, those who fall from a cliff or mountainside, women who die in childbirth, all may feel rage and envy for the living and cause them harm, possessing them and "eating" their vital energy so they waste away and finally die. "Look," said a woman at the stream while we were standing in line with our water jugs, forest boughs overhanging and the ferns growing up near the rocks. She pointed at the place where the path ran along near the cliff. "This is where Gyan's wife fell. She grabbed at me as she went down but I held back. I would have died, too." I looked over and saw the chasm going down to the rocks below. Frightened, I stepped away, imagining what it must have been like to fall, the horror of those moments in space.

There is a special name for the spirits of those who die from falling, *bir*, and people fear them. A malevolent being might once have been a neighbor or friend, now a spirit caught in limbo and corroded with rage. After any death it is believed that the spirit wanders the village for three days, not knowing it has died. It approaches people and wonders why they do not respond. It is hungry and wonders why it has no food. There is no space made on the mat when it enters. At night the doors are bolted and it is left out in the dark. Desperate, it rattles doors and pounds on windows, but the living do not respond. On the third morning after the death, offerings are made and the spirit is informed that it is no longer a living being, a fact it accepts with resistance and dismay, as it makes its way to the next life. Those who die an untoward death remain near. Not relinquishing their clinging to life and consumed with bitterness, they in turn consume the vulnerable.

A witch is said to "eat" her victims. Like dangerous spirits live on the edge of life, witches live on the edge of society. It is against the law to name someone as a witch, so nothing was ever mentioned to me about witches for a long time. After I had lived in the village for a year, I thought I might make a solitary retreat for a couple of days in an abandoned house just a little into the forest. Ama was horrified. It was comparable to saying I wanted to go stay alone in a cheap hotel in south-central Los Angeles for a couple of days. Only instead of drive-by shootings, pimps, and crack vendors, there were various crafty or vicious beings, spirits and agents of witches. She sat me down and told me that unsavory things wander in the forest and come near villages looking to do harm. She said there were witches in the village. To be alone there, at the vulnerable edge of the forest was to be almost certain of being attacked, she told me.

I was shocked. I had heard people refer to witches, and talk of illnesses caused by them, but to imagine an immediate danger of witches within the village astonished me. Ama continued. She led me onto the veranda and pointed out a row of houses, one lineage. "The mother is a witch," she said, "and so are the daughters and the daughters-in-law."

"But don't the daughters-in-law come from other families?" I asked.

"Yes," she replied, "witch families. They bring women in marriage from the households of other witches. We do not shun them. We are always polite if they come by, and you should be, too. It is foolish to offend a witch. But spend as little time with those women as possible." They were not people I knew well, so this was not a problem. "There is another old woman at the top of the village," she said, and told me that the woman chose to live away from the other households and near the forest, so that she could cultivate witch-familiars.

Tson joined the conversation and told me of how her father, a lama, had made a witch confess from inside the patient's body. She said her voice was fearsome and that she shrieked with rage and pain. "My father held a red-hot rice pot to the patient's cheek to force the witch to speak," Tson said.

"Didn't that hurt the patient?" I asked.

"Not at all. It didn't leave a mark," she replied. "It hurt the witch. Nowadays the king says you must not call anyone a witch. You can be put in jail. But in the old days you could find them and make them stop. You know the old shaman, the one who did the big ritual you went to in Torr, when his mother and brother died?"

"Yes, I remember. It was when I got sick."

"Well, he was a powerful exorcist and finally he was killed by a witch. You know the old woman who lives in Torr by the water tap, with the big goiter? She ate him and he died. Someone saw her, sitting by the water tap and stroking his body. She just ate up his life. Don't go stay up by the forest."

It was getting dark and shadows had fallen across the slopes on the other side of the gorge. We saw a brief red flicker, like a tiny spark, across in the dusk. "Witches' fire," Ama said. "They go out of the village and make fires for their rituals." Bunti and Seyli returned with baskets of fodder on their backs and the rap of hooves on the flagstone mingled with the sound of bells let us know the herding boy was back with the goats. It was time for dinner. We rose and I followed Tson and Ama into the house.

"Why do witches attack people?" I asked Katwale once. He was kind to me and I liked him.

"Because the victim has something that the witch wants. She might see you eating and think, 'Mmm. I'd like some of that.' You might not even realize she was there, much less know that she was hungry, but because you had the food and did not give her any, she would do you harm," he replied.

He had treated me once or twice when Ama felt there was something unnatural about the way an illness lingered on. I would open my shawl for him to blow mantras at my midriff or sit very still while he brushed a burning broom across my body. The illnesses still seemed to linger. "Mmm, tenacious witch," he would say, and try again, heading down to the crossroads with a miniature meal on the leaf plate. After a time I got better.

Gopal, Badhay's youngest son was home for several months on leave and liked to spend time at our house. I was working in the evening once, trying to finish some writing before I went to sleep, and some teenagers came by, yet again wanting to sit in my room.

"Not now," I said. "I really need to finish this writing."

"So write," they said. "We'll just sit and talk."

"No," I replied, and turned back to my work. It is rude to refuse anything to anyone directly, and I was again failing at civility. Gopal came to the window after they left.

"You should be more polite," he said.

"But they always come around, and the children," I said. "I get so tired of it."

"You don't want to make people angry," he replied. "You never know who might be a witch. Witches wash their hair at night at the big pool by the stream. Have you ever seen them?"

"No," I answered.

"And there is a shaman in the forest. He lives behind a waterfall deep in the jungle. He has lived there for hundreds of years. He kidnaps boys to be his disciples. I stayed with him once for a while. He can teach mantras so that you can make a girl fall in love and sleep with you." He looked at me and smiled. I arranged my shawl. "Would you like to become a witch?" he asked.

"No," I said. "I don't want to learn how to hurt people." He sauntered across the courtyard, and I lit a candle and wrote for a while more.

People moved freely there, not restricted to paths and trails. They approached windows, traversed courtyards, crossed thresholds. Boundaries restrained untouchables: these were formal rules, set in place by the royal government more than a century before. The untouchables were prohibited from crossing the thresholds of Gurung houses and using some water-taps but mainly people of all castes wandered free, the mosaic of court-yards and paths providing order but not constraining.

The poor wandered more than others. Muna was an old woman who looked like every picture of a witch I had ever seen in fairy-tale books. She was bent and old with a large hooked nose and stringy gray hair. Her home was a windowless room that had been used for storage. I first met her when I initially arrived and had been unable to finish the great heap of rice on my plate. I felt bad to see it wasted but I was full. Ama took my plate and handed it to a someone in the shadows. It was Muna. I saw her bent fingers scoop up the rice and heard her slurping the accompanying vegetables. I was shocked since eating food from another's plate is considered completely disgusting in Nepal. Pajon told me that when she had seen tourists eat one another's food, it had made her gag and nearly vomit. Women take their husband's leftovers to show their submission and to affirm that for them (though not the man) intimacy overrides disgust. A mother will also take her child's leftovers. Children do not defile in the same way as adults, and as in marriage, a mother's love overcomes disgust. Intimate friends may also share one another's food, using the idiom of the rule to show their affection: "As in a child or a mate, what might defile from others does not from you." Abject poverty also overcomes disgust, so for Muna everyone was an intimate.

Muna's beaked nose was the only visible marker she had of her descent from the warrior caste, second only to Brahmins in the Hindu ranking system. She had come to the village in middle age as a destitute widow and been taken in as a servant, doing errands and odd jobs for wealthier families in village. There was a grown son who had joined the Indian army but she had not heard from him in many years, and worried that he had died. People murmured that he did not want to be bothered with her, but she could not imagine such betrayal. She was now too old to work, so begged foodstuffs and leftovers from people's houses. Ama and Apa gave her the storage room to sleep in and we could hear her singing devotional songs at night when the doors were open. "Witches' mantras," one mean-spirited teenager said of them, when the words drifted out with the smoke from her fire of sticks, but no one that I knew believed her to be a witch. She gathered her sticks in the day and would perform small tasks for Ama, like washing dishes. She came to my room from time to time, always unobtrusive and polite. I had a decorated thermos that I had gotten cheap in the bazaar in Kathmandu. It was covered with pictures from Zefferelli's film *Romeo and Juliet*. I was always a little embarrassed by their immodest embraces, but Muna loved to look at it, and would hold it and gaze at all the details. "So sweet," she sighed one day, "the mother and son."

On warm days she would sit in her rags in the courtyard sunning herself. Village children played there, too. One day I was walking through to Leela's. The morning had been cool, but now the sun had risen high enough to warm the courtyard. Ama and Tson were out and the door to the house was bolted. Muna had been sitting in the sun and some eight- or nine-year-old boys had come and were throwing stones at her. Their mothers, the Magar woman and two or three others, were chatting nearby. Muna crouched and tried to shield herself with her hand.

"Look," I said to the women, "see what the boys are doing."

"What does it matter?" one replied and they continued their conversation. The boys continued to pelt her.

"Stop that!" I told them, getting upset. "It is a bad thing to do." Their mothers turned and beckoned the children away.

"Who is she to you," one said, "that you should care?" The words echoed in my ears. Without status and relationship, you were no one. I was young, from a wealthy country, adopted by the headman's family, but I might have been her. Once when I walked through an unknown village, boys threw rocks at me. It was terrifying. I told Leela what had happened in the courtyard and about the women's unresponsiveness. "They didn't care at all," I said sadly. She laid her hand on my knee. "They have small heart-minds," she said.

The style of brutality has changed over time. People still fear witches, but they also tell stories about the acts of disaffected young men. Violence has always been there. It is a tension under the harmonious surface of day-to-day life, mostly repressed, but erupting from time to time, feeding the focused fury for which the Gurkha soldiers are famous. People are fascinated with violence and tell stories of death in great detail: the children who burned in the house fire, their little charred bones found in the ashes; the grandmother who went out for a pee, tottered over, panted, and died. Then there are the famous stories, told over and over, like the one about the village across the gorge from Torr where an old woman lived in the house of her son, a soldier who had invested heavily in gold, with her teenage granddaughter. They had been slaughtered with khukuris, the curved knives used by Gurkhas. "The granddaughter must have fought furiously," they said; "the house was sprayed with blood. She really wanted to live." I imagined the soft clay walls of the house laced with red, like a scene from *Macbeth*. Neighbors had seen the bodies through the latticed window. People took it to be a crime of vicious outsiders but later learned the murderers were relatives who lived on an adjoining terrace. The thought of the gold in a small trunk under the bed had tempted them to do the unthinkable, killing family for greed.

This was an old story when I came there. Later, on return trips as the years passed, stories of violence were more frequent and more sordid. There were accounts of young men hungry for the glamor they had witnessed at the cinema hall in town, with enough education to despise farm work but no prospects beyond it, jealous of the shiny possessions of tourists, who lurked in the forest and killed travelers or raped local girls. Three beautiful teenage girls picnicking at a lake near Pokhara had been raped and murdered by boys from Kathmandu, one a rejected suitor of the loveliest. From a wealthy family, he was not used to being refused, and she had declined a formal marriage proposal on account of his bad character. A tourist girl was robbed and killed on the trail beyond Melori by a young man from town who had befriended her. Even in nearby Sohrya, a tough village boy had trapped a girl in the schoolroom at night threatening to rape her. When her younger brother pleaded with him to spare his sister, the teenage boy had beaten him till he collapsed, and he had died the next day while being taken by his parents to the hospital.

These stories captured the imagination of people and mingled with tales of evil spirits and witches. Some mothers (the more forward-looking ones) threatened their children not with the figure of the ghost or jackal, but with the criminal or policeman who would carry them off if they did not finish their dinner right away. When I first told Ama of the muggings and indiscriminate violence that took place in America, trying to correct the view that I had come from paradise, she had shaken her head bemusedly and said, "There must be so many crazy people there." As time went on, there seemed to be more crazy, overt malice in Nepal, too.

Witches and evil spirits fit an ordered universe, in a strange way, even as they undermine it. They embody (with or without bodies) what is left out of the gracious, harmonious world that people strive to create. Everyone knows that world is not real. Everyone suffers exclusion and pain. The scenario of the spirit on the edge of human life, hungry, longing, and filled with resentment speaks to the real experience and real fears of living people. Nurture and inclusion are the motifs of Gurung social life, but who can be flawlessly sustained and completely enveloped in anything short of the womb? Who can endlessly sustain others? Yet the illusion is so beguiling. To enter a household is to be offered food, and the plate is filled and refilled until the sated eater covers it and protests, "Enough, enough." The promise of more is always there. When a person walks through the village, everyone she encounters will call out to her: "O, younger sister!" "O, elder sister!" O, granddaughter!" invoking the proper kin term, whether real or contrived. There is a deep sense of belonging in this, the lapping of a warm sea of acknowledgment. There is also a structure in it, the architecture of kinship created and recreated in each encounter through the day, orienting a person to life: "This is the human world. This is who I am related to. This is who I am." There is comfort in it, and grace. One is specific and whole, but like a jewel held up to the sun, a different facet of the self shows in each encounter: "Now I am a sister, now a child, now a mother," and each connection is a link to the larger whole. This is both real and unreal, a truth-of-the-moment and a beautiful artifice.

As Buddhists, Gurungs believe the reality we inhabit is provisional and that it both expresses and obscures the larger truth of life. The cozy world in which everyone belongs does exist, and is actualized at moments in everyone's lives, but its dark side, revealing it as illusion, is also true and real. The social world with its extravagant promises is bound to disappoint. People withhold goods and favors, not with direct refusal, but with lies: "We don't have any." "I wish I could help, but I made another promise that day." It is more polite to lie than to say no. The surface is smooth but suspicions run underneath: "I am sure they had sugar, but they did not want to give us any." People are not sure what they can rely on when words are used to create harmony rather than accurately convey intentions: "He said he would come help us today. Maybe he will and maybe he won't. We will know when he shows up." Truth unfolds in actuality. The value of words is uncertain until the event occurs. Behavior is what counts.

Young children are trained in generosity before they can talk. A toddler will be told to give up a cherished object, a little stick or a nice piece of food, coaxed and cajoled, with the family looking on and a large adult looming over with hand extended, smiling and saying, "for your grandfather, that's a good boy." The child hands it over, looking tense and unhappy, and the receiver and others praise him extravagently, then return it, at which point the child seems gratified, but clings to it uneasily, looking around. Anyone can ask for your belongings. It is rude to say no, so excuses must be made, or giving deferred to some nonexistent future, or insincere promises offered forth. Sometimes mothers challenge the ultimate attachment, playfully offering the breast to another child while the nursing toddler stands by, "You won't mind if I give Chon some milk, will you." The child stands there glowering and silent while the circle of young women laugh in the sun. The mother then lifts her own child and gives him the breast, soothing his rage.

An old woman asks me if I will take her to America, and I patiently explain that I have only one ticket and cannot buy another, trying to convey the vast cost in Nepalese rupees of a plane ticket to go so far. After she leaves, Ama, exasperated, looks at me across the fire and explains, "Don't say no to her. It isn't nice. Do you think that old woman wants to go to America? She never even goes out of the village. Say to her, 'Of course, Grandmother. I'll let you know when it's time so you can pack your things. We'll have fun in my country.' That's more polite." There is deception, playful and not. There are undercurrents of rage. The social universe is warm, attractive, and often sustaining, but it is deeply and frighteningly untrustworthy. Out of the fault lines in the surface of this harmonious world arise envy, resentment, malice, erupting in the figures of the evil spirit and the witch, secretly consuming what they were not given, the life force of others; and the image of the modern criminal, harming others in a frenzy of rage.

These are figures on the margins, at the same time as they may be intimates. Margins are threatening and strange. Twilight is the time when the lamas send the spirit to the afterlife, and when shamans make offerings at the crossroads. The bereaved, seen as at the edge of life and death, are set apart, excluded from community rituals until the funeral has cleansed them of the taint of death. The edge of the village near the forest is unsafe; uncanny things lurk in the bamboo grove at its boundary. The new mother, too near the mystery of birth, cannot be touched. The center must be kept intact, the illusion of ongoing life and complete integration protected, continuity and wholeness celebrated and threat held at bay by the lamas and the shamans, who contain disruption and impose order. Who knows what causes evil? Planets out of conjunction bring misfortune or vulnerability to harm. Bad actions in a previous life bear fruit in this one, creating an unfortunate destiny. Space and time collapse into the present moment when the witch walks by bringing that destiny to pass as someone eats on the veranda.

Bhayo lived at the edge of the village, on a terrace opening out on the fields running down to the river, the fields where the Phalgun full moon was celebrated. Not far above it was the entrance to the forest. Her house was small, mud and thatch like Mallum's house, with a little courtyard. She lived alone. Her name meant "all done," a message to the gods from her mother, for whom she had been the fourteenth child. She lived just a little way from the headman's house and used to come through our courtyard from time to time. I found her intriguing. She ignored me. Her gray hair stuck out from her round wrinkled face. She was definitely not sweet and she was definitely eccentric. Her eyes were small and fierce and she carried a rough staff that was taller than she was. The children in my family addressed her as Bhayo Bhuju, Grandmother All Done, and invited her to stay and chat when she was not busy harvesting her little bit of crops or bringing sticks for her fire. She had never married but was given a small portion of land and her house by her brother. One day Agai combed her hair for her as we all sat on mats in the sun oiling and braiding each other's hair. "See how pretty it looks," said Agai, handing her a small mirror. Bhayo Bhuju squinted at the mirror and assented.

"You should comb it from time to time," said Agai.

"What for?" said Bhayo Bhuju as she handed her back the mirror and lay down on the mat.

Occasionally I would come home and find her lying on a mat in the house like a mannikin tipped on its back, holding her staff, and carrying on a conversation with Ama as she cooked. Her hair was a silver mane against the straw mat and her voice and face were animated as she spoke. Ama listened and nodded and peeled potatoes.

In spite of her living on the margins in every way and her raggedy insolent strangeness, no one took Bhayo Bhuju to be a witch. She did, however, have some problems with the supernatural. It came of living at the edge, people said. When there are numbers of people around, uncanny beings stay away. But Bhayo Bhuju's house was by itself on a terrace, looking down on a cascade of fields and the river, with the forest not far above it. She came tapping her staff across the courtyard one day and announced in exasperation, "They're back."

"What? What's back?" I asked Seyli, sitting a little aside drinking tea.

"The forest men," Seyli said. "She's been having a terrible problem with them."

I had learned about the forest men when Seyli told me she had refused to meet a friend at the winter tea stall on the rice fields.

"There is no way I would walk through the forest alone," she said. "I might be attacked by a forest man."

"What's a forest man?" I asked.

"They live in the forest," she replied.

"Mmm." I said.

"They are smaller than us," she continued, "and hairy all over, with red faces. And their feet are on backward. They are dangerous. If even their shadow touches you, you will fall ill. And if your shadow falls across the forest man, he will become ill." Her voice quieted. "They like women and if they find you alone they will rape you, and if a woman is raped by a forest man, she will go crazy, or shrink to the size of a thumb."

"Oh," I said, startled at the thought.

Bhimsen had told me, in Cliff Shelter with the river singing in the background, that forest men sometimes approached men, hungry for the comforts of human habitation, and begged to live alongside them in the house, promising riches and power in return. For a while the wealth of the household would grow and the forest man remain humble and grateful (and always out of sight). Then the power of the man would fade little by little and the forest man would control everything. He said forest men might also do the bidding of witches.

Though alien and dangerous, the forest men are also the closest of intimates. A learned lama, abbot of a small monastery to the north who stopped in the village to visit, took me aside and asked if it was true what he had heard about Western ideas of human origins. "I have heard that your caste also believes that humans are descended from monkeys," he said with excitement. "Could you tell me about that?" I gave him a rough sketch of the theory of evolution. "Ah," he said. "It is similar! We believe that humans come from a monkey father and a forest woman mother, and that we were given the capacity for wisdom by the bodhisattva of compassion."

However wide and varied the beliefs, stories about the forest man were most often told by fearful young women, their positions insecure since they could at any time be snatched from their homes by a party of men and given in marriage, their tenuousness of place giving the lie to slurpy sweet scenarios of belonging, integration, and harmony. According to the lamas, we embody the greed, lust, and aggression envisioned in the stories of forest men, the primal drives bred in human blood and bone (though our most essential being is pure). According to the young women, lust and aggression lurk about ready to intrude and destroy the wholeness of their lives, a transformation they do not welcome, avoiding the forest, evading desire.

Bhayo Bhuju, never having married, was permanently on the margins. To marry is to be ripped out of your home and knitted into another one. But if a girl stays in her cherished home it will unravel and reconfigure around her. Parents die. Sisters are carried off to husband's homes. Brothers bring wives and have children, creating their own households. An unmarried sister is a nuisance. Another old unmarried sister in the village was sent to live in the stable when her brother wanted her small house for his son. She came to me with tears running down her wrinkled face and asked if I would send a note for her to the king, telling him of her brother's wrongs. "Let His Majesty know," she said. "Perhaps he will help me." Bhayo's brother was good to her. He had never married either, and they were the only surviving children of all the many their mother had borne. She stayed in the village where she had grown up, but her home was little and vulnerable.

Bhayo leaned on her staff in the courtyard and told us she had had another sleepless night. "It is bad enough that they come in the day and try to make love with me. They sneak into my house and hide in the attic, then come down when I return. I chased several out with a broom. But now at night they come, too." Atay, Ama, and Tson murmured their sympathy. Bunti and Seyli, now ripe adolesents, looked at each other and leaned closer together. I listened and wondered. After some time, village teenagers were sent to sleep with Bhayo in her small house to protect her against the creatures. "I did not see them," Seyli said when she had gone to help. "But I heard them scuffling around outside. I was so scared it gave me chills." I thought of pretty Seyli lying there in the dark, starlight on the fields and noises outside, hearing the rasp of the old woman's sleepy breathing, as she wondered if the forest men would penetrate her fragile shelter.

- learning how family came to honor.
- becoming part of family
- good daughter
5. - realizing that she's not Gurung

Paths Without a Compass: Learning Family

Danger can enter even houses bolted against it. We went as a family to Torr, out of the village on the slippery path past the stream, through the forest that climbed up the steep slope, the trees opening to narrow waterfalls tumbling down, hewn log footbridges set across the flowing water where it met the path. After a while the forest opened onto fields. Travel was slow. We walked quickly, but each time we came to a settlement, we were called in for tea by friends or relatives. Apa would protest but they would insist (protesting and insisting are always part of social calls) and up we would go to the steps of the veranda. Bundles would be set down and we would file into the dim house, sitting in order of precedence: Apa nearest the altar, Ama after him, me next to Ama, then Seyli. Maila and Bunti had stayed behind to look after the household and the smaller children with Tson. People in the area were accustomed to me by then, so I was not the center of attention, but sat quietly by after speaking a little in Gurung and Nepali to show off Ama's good training. The fact that I spoke, dressed, and conducted myself properly accrued to her honor and that of the family, just as my failures would diminish it. As we approached a village, she would prime me: "Now we will stop at our relatives' house. You must call the woman 'father's-middle-born-sister' (Panni). Call the man 'husband-of-older-female-relative-on the-father's-side' (Aumo)." These might be distant cousins, since the terms reflected very broad categories, but the intimate and precise language created a sense of closeness. When I greeted them properly, they looked pleased. I felt happy at those moments.

Our slow progress brought us to Sohrya at evening. We called at the house of an old man and woman, who insisted that we stay. Some could sleep in the house, they said, and others in the room above the stable. The house was small but had a wide, walled courtyard, a little mill house, and a large room with a carved window above the stable. They were both erect and composed, and the woman had large, soft eyes. She was wearing a maroon brocade blouse and had a small diamond in her nose. Their son was away in the British army. "Sit," she said to me, patting a place next to her on the mat. I was excited when they told me that many years before, in their youth, a French anthropologist had stayed with them. This must have been Bernard Pignède, a famous student of Gurung culture from Paris who was in Nepal at about that time. I had read his book. "He was agreeable," the old man said. "He shared his food and played his tape machine for us." I looked across the courtyard at the room he had stayed in and imagined him cooking his food there. I wondered what people would say of me in thirty years. "She was nice *sometimes*," perhaps, or "She could carry a lot." I looked out at the fading light and continued to daydream. The old woman passed me a plate of popcorn and some tea and I turned back to the conversation.

The old woman was speaking, her voice low and intent. "My son's father (her husband) was away and it was just me and my daughter-in-law and the schoolmaster who boarded with us," she said. "We were all sleeping, the doors and windows bolted. Then in the middle of the night, a large cat jumped down from the meat-drying rack above the fire. It went for the schoolmaster, but he threw an altarpiece at it. I woke and saw it hissing fire. It leapt then onto my daughter-in-law, and she cried out and then fell back. The cat vanished. It was gone. When we went over to my daughter-in-law, she was dead." Tears trickled down her face. Ama looked at her sadly. Everyone was quiet. The old man stared at the fire. I looked at the wooden cot against the wall where the young woman had slept, quilts rolled neatly at the end. They put me in the room above the stable to sleep that night. I lay in bed and looked through the latticed window at the stars above the mountains, inch by inch between the wooden frames. A witch had sent the cat, the old woman had said. Some sort of retribution. I pulled my quilts more tightly around me and closed my eyes. The strangeness of the story, its improbability in a rational world, and the fact of the woman's death chased each other in my mind.

In the morning we continued on to Torr. We were out of the jungle now and followed a stone path to the fields. Some were lying fallow and some were soft with the new green of growing barley. We were walking toward the Himals but they were veiled by curling white and gray clouds, the white ones wispy and the gray ones fat and ample. Apa walked in front, brisk with his shorts and neat, straight walking stick. This gorge ascended from Cliff Shelter where the fierce, swift Dimrod river that came down from the Annapurnas met the lazy Kumrum that flowed below Tebas. Looking back, we could see the tiny shape of Bhimsen's lodge in the valley and the small suspension bridge that rocked and swayed as people crossed to the steep cliff on the other side. The gorge opened up like a cornucopia, spilling out the buildings and green fields lower down. Beyond Cliff Shelter, the river spread into the melting hills. We continued up. The land here was rough and rocky. The terraces were small, hardly room for a bullock to turn with the plow. The path was bordered by a rock wall that supported the fields above it. Below was open and steep. Great black vultures with ragged wings dipped down into the gorge, skimmed below us, and swept up again. Apa's walking stick tapped the stone as he swung it jauntily while he walked. Ama's dark blue sari was pulled tight around her hips and her rubber slippers slapped the path as she walked behind him with short quick steps. I watched her thin body ahead of me, enjoying the sensation of being placed between her and Seyli, our steps in rhythm, as though we were all part of one creature, family as organism snaking along the trail. Ama held her head high and her braid fell straight between her shoulder blades, a black ribbon woven into it. I had woven a red one into my hair, like Seyli, and wore a beige sari of crunchy stiff cotton with red and blue peacocks along its border. I padded along in soft cloth shoes. Ama had put two gold bracelets on my wrist, marked with curved points like the waves of the sea. They were beautiful and made my arm heavy. We passed three *chorten*, stone shrines marking the approach to Torr. I could see white houses, small in the distance, their smooth slate roofs gleaming in the sun.

The gorge narrowed there and led into the Annapurna basin, well beyond Torr. Maila lama had told me that monks went up to meditate in caves in the great amphitheater formed by the ring of mountains in hope that they might be blessed with the presence of the goddess who dwelled there. The thrusting rock that showed when the clouds parted looked forbidding. I imagined the snow valley beautiful and white. Pajon had told me of a party of French trekkers swept away by an avalanche there. The Sherpa guides were able to dig all of them out except the young wife of a man on his honeymoon. Pajon said he wept without stopping when they came down to the inn, and she remembered the fresh-faced woman with brown eyes who had been kind to the children when they went up, so happy. He came back in the spring with a helicopter and they found her body, perfect in the ice, and brought her back to France.

Apa had some business, not explained to me, to conduct in Torr. We called in first at Tson's birth home. Their hamlet was called Lower Village. It was beyond even Siva's inn, near the drop-off that sheered into the gorge, a little apart from the main mass of Torr. Hidden by a slope that rose above it, Lower Village nestled in a curving oval of land like the bowl of a spoon, and looked up at the mountains, being nearest them of all the village. The path was smooth and perfect, paved with stones, and the houses were substantial. The path dipped down a bit, then climbed up toward the little plateau. Tson's house was at the edge, a wooden gateway marking her courtyard. As I passed through it, I thought of her standing at the threshold years before watching the marriage party come, and wished that she had been able to accompany us.

The courtyard was broad, enclosed by a wall, and in the corner was a stable with a room above it, reached by wooden steps. Her mother greeted us. Tendrils of her gray hair curled around her temples. Tson was her youngest child. She invited us in. There is a certain formality between in-laws, so the talk was polite and subdued. Seyli sat at the edge of the mat with her hands in her lap. We were given special fried bread, like doughnuts, and thick milky tea. Little brass dishes of savory potatoes were set before us by a girl about twelve, her hair thick and black, like Tson's. She was Tson's niece, her older brother's child. We all sat quietly with our food in front of us until Tson's mother urged us to eat. Hungry after the walk, the food tasted especially good. The round sweet bread was made of rice flour and had a slight grainy texture and the potatoes were pleasantly spicy. The old woman gave us more, then offered us more again, but Apa said we needed to leave so we could reach the upper village before dark. As we were going, Tson's brother came, tall and broad-shouldered, wearing a white shirt and a white Gurung kilt pulled snug around his body, prayer beads around his neck marking his position as a lama. "Going so soon?" he said. His breath smelled slightly of liquor.

We climbed up the back way to the upper village. The path was unpaved, a narrow grassy track that was used to bring animals out to pasture. As we reached the houses people called out greetings. We continued on and entered the path that wound between the houses, bounded by walls on either side and paved with stones. These were marked by the droppings of the buffaloes that were being driven home from pasture, slippery splotches that we edged around. We stopped at Pajon's to greet her and drop off my bundle. Anna came out into the courtyard when she heard us, and asked after her parents.

"You are looking well," she said to me, "not so thin." She turned to Ama and Apa. "We thought she would die here, so sick and not eating a thing. She has good color now." Her younger daughter and Seyli were chatting in the corner. We went into Pajon's house and she directed Apa to put my bundle on the cot near the fire. I would stay alone there with her, so there would not be such a houseful at Ama's birth home, but I would go ahead with the rest of the family for dinner.

*   *   *

Torr was Ama's clan home. She sometimes said to me, "You are a Plun woman's daughter." The Plun were a great clan, and Torr was their stronghold. Apa was a Kon, the leading clan of Tebas. There were many intermarriages between the two. I was excited to think of meeting Ama's mother. Her father, now dead, had been from a high ranking lineage and had also become quite wealthy as a trader and moneylender. He was clever, Ama said, and ruthless.

"Your father's father, the old headman, would let debts go. He was kind, but his money dwindled. My father collected, and with interest. He brought in every rupee and more. He grew very rich." We were sitting in the courtyard at home, just the two of us. Tson was milling rice, and the rest were in the fields or off to the forest to cut wood. "My mother could not have children," Ama said, "the mother who raised me. My father loved her, though, and would not divorce her. But he brought another wife, the mother who bore me. You know the mother who came with the man I called 'younger brother' from Khum? They had tea and talked with us in the courtyard? That was the mother who bore me. It made the first wife very unhappy to have her in the house, so she was sent away, back to her parents. He arranged to meet her in the jungle sometimes, though, and they made love but there were no more children. I stayed with my father and the elder mother. She did everything for me, even as a little baby: cleaned my shit, fed me. How could I not call her mother? She was very good to me, just as though I were her own. After a while the second wife, the one from whose womb I came, married someone else and went to live in Khum. She gave birth to that tall man; he is her son. She liked to run around and have fun; she didn't care about me one bit. I never saw her.

"At home, I was the only child in the house until I was twelve. My father treated me like a son. He taught me to ride; he talked to me about his plans and ideas. Then another woman came, a new wife. My elder mother cried. The new wife had a son, my younger brother who lives in Torr, but his mother died when he was born. My mother raised him. She is very loving. I was married when I was twelve and my father gave me the house in Tebas. For my brother, there was the house in Torr, and two more houses in town, so he thought that would be enough for him. This big house is mine, and several fields here." She gestured to the land below the village.

"I was married to your father's elder brother first, the second son. He was handsome and very kind. Everyone admired him. Even when I was little, he used to laugh and say that he would marry me. He was eighteen when we were married, and went off to the Second World War. He died in the fighting. His mother nearly died of grief, crying and not eating. He had been her favorite, and her youngest son had died abroad too, not of a wound but of an abscessed tooth. The British said I could keep my husband's pension until I married again, but if I married his brother, it would be mine for life. So our families arranged that I should marry the third brother, and he became the headman, your father, as his older brother would have been. Come. Let's go make the tea. The others will be back for their snack soon." I thought of the times I found Apa genially making the morning snack, saying "Your mother is busy. I can do a bit of everything," and the way their legs sometimes touched when they thought no one was watching. I wondered about the shadowy, glamorous figure behind them, lying dead on the battlefield so long ago.

Ama got up and I rolled up the mat on the courtyard and followed her past the carved porch pillars into the dim house. She placed little sticks against the coals and blew on them a bit. The ashes flew up. I took over, coaxing the heat with my breath until a coal began to glow. I held my hair back, kneeling, and continued to blow on the coals, focusing my breath on the warm red center of the fire pit. Finally the kindling caught, and little flames lapped at the wood. Ama rearranged the sticks and placed the kettle on top, then went to the pantry to get some potatoes. Shafts of light came through the latticed window onto her mat, illumining the drifting smoke.

*　　*　　*

Smoke was rising from houses in Torr as we made our way to Ama's brother's house at evening time. Pajon urged me to come back early. We walked through the stone pathways in a line, seeing the soft light of lamps and firelight against the clay walls inside the houses we passed. People sat round their fires ready for a meal. When we entered the house, Ama bowed low, placing her head on her mother's feet.

"May you be well; may your heart be strong; may you have long life," said her mother in blessing. Apa and Seyli bowed, and I did, too. "So this is the white grandchild," she said, taking my hand. "Stay well here."

"I am happy to be able to pay my respects to our grandmother," I replied. She smiled. She was beautiful, with soft hair completely white and lovely features. Her skin was delicately wrinkled, like parchment.

"Sit. Eat. My son has gone to town with his boy and I am here with my daughter-in-law and my granddaughter," she said. A woman with a round face and fair skin who had greeted us at the door stirred some pots by the fire and a girl peeked out from behind her. Ama sat beside her mother and the old woman rested her hand on Ama's knee. We arranged ourselves on mats and large brass plates were set before us. The plates were heaped with rice and in small brass bowls around it were succulent goat meat and sauteed greens, lentils in rich broth and fried potatoes. The meal was delicious. We ate silently, hungry after the long walk. I liked the food sounds: a slurp of lentils, the plop of more rice being served, the question "More?" followed by acquiescent murmurs. The fragrant smoke mixed with the food aromas and a few flames leapt as the wood pieces burned down. I felt perfectly contented. I listened quietly and leaned my back against the firm wooden cot behind me as I watched the fire for a while. The melody of voices speaking Gurung lulled me into sleepiness, then I remembered Pajon.

"I should go," I said. "Pajon is waiting."

"We have bedding enough here for all our granddaughters," said Ama's mother.

"Indeed," I replied, "and it would be pleasant to stay, but Pajon has invited me and said she would wait up."

"Go well, then," said the grandmother. I bowed to her.

"Sleep well, then. We'll see you tomorrow," said Ama sitting beside her mother, relaxed with their knees touching.

The little girl stepped out with me to show me the way. White peaks were visible under the stars and moonlight washed the pale courtyards on the terrace below. A breeze rustled a stand of bamboo as we stepped onto the path. The child clicked on the flashlight and its round circle of light guided us on the uneven stones.

Pajon was washing her dishes at the edge of her porch when we arrived, rubbing a paste of ashes into the metal dishes and rinsing them into a small square pit below. A kerosene lamp burned next to her as she worked.

"O Pajon," I called in greeting.

"You've come," she replied. She rinsed the last few dishes and stacked them, gleaming and wet. The little girl leaned against the pillar and watched, the tip of her shawl touching the ground. When Pajon rose to go in, she turned and walked back toward the path.

"Go well, child," I called after her. She glanced back and grinned, then flipped the edge of her shawl over her shoulder and walked quickly on.

"Come," said Pajon. I followed her into the house. She set the lamp on the ledge below the altar. The flame made the clay walls glow. I sat on the mat under soft scarlet outlines of the hanging Buddha image. Pajon stirred the coals and poked some fresh sticks in and small flames began to lick them. She placed the kettle on the tripod. "We'll have tea," she said. She got up and poured a glass of milk from the pantry. When the kettle boiled, she poured the dark, sweet tea into our glasses, then the milk, making it rich and creamy.

"Do you have buffaloes in your country?" she asked.

"No, just cows," I replied.

"Too bad," she said. "Cow's milk is so thin. Did you stop along the way here?"

"Yes, all the time. We stopped twice in Tansen for tea and spent the night in Sohrya. Then we stopped at Tson's for tea. When I come alone it is just half a day's walk."

"When people have honor, like your mother and father, they have to stop or others will be offended."

"I didn't mind," I said. "It was pleasant. How have you been?"

"My joints hurt lately," she said. "Kancha lama came today and gave me an amulet and some medicine. Siva thinks lama medicine is useless but it does help. He only believes in the shots and pills that the doctors give. The shots helped me, but I cannot get them here. The lama's medicine helps, too. Kancha lama knows a great deal and takes a good care of me."

"I don't know Kancha lama," I said. "Is he from the high mountains or nearby?"

"He is one of our Gurung lamas, not a northerner," she replied. "You can trust the Gurung lamas. They have families; they live like the rest of us."

"What about the northerners?" I asked.

"Them? Those northerners don't marry. They claim to be monks but they cast their eyes at women. If there is a daughter in the house where they are doing a ritual, you have to watch them."

"Really?" I said. I thought about Prema lama. Ama had introduced me to him when I first came. He was the ritual friend of a soldier away in the army, and lived with the soldier's elderly mother in a house near ours. When I said I wished to study Buddhism, Ama arranged for me to study with him. He was a northerner and had taken a vow of celibacy. He wore full maroon robes and was handsome, with long dark eyes. I went down to their house to work with him on the Tibetan script and Buddhist thought for about an hour each morning when he was around the village, but he was often away. I was sometimes unsettled by the way he looked at me but was flattered by his warm attention and touched by his kindness. "What about Prema lama?" I said. "You know, the one who lives with Nam Bahadur's mother?"

"He is just like that," she answered.

"He is?" I asked.

"He is. He lived here for a while, in Torr. He has many ritual friends. It's interesting that most of them are soldiers. You know those gold rings, he wears?" Prema lama wore three large gold rings on his hands, yellow against his coppery skin. "It's not proper for a lama. He buys things cheap from his ritual friends, the goods soldiers bring home from abroad to make a little money. Then he sells them in town. You may have wondered why he travels so much. He always stays with his ritual friends, never paying them a cent or bringing a gift, but he is so charming. The man knows how to talk. His friends here finally told him to leave and he went to Tebas. No one likes him there, except that old woman."

"Ama seems to like him," I said. "He often stops in."

"Your mother is polite to him but she does not like him. You know that dark woman, the one who lives a little ways above you? She has a daughter."

"Yes, I know her. She goes to Prema's room for medicine sometimes."

"Well," Pajon continued, "Prema lama built that house for her. It's a strange place, with two rooms, like a house in the bazaar. He goes there at night and stays with her. Her husband came back once a few years ago, but since then he stays in India. He does not want her now."

I was shocked. I remembered that I had met them at an inn on my way down to Cliff Shelter a few weeks earlier. She was sleeping in a separate shelter and he had gone that way, too, after dark. I thought of the little gifts he had given me and his even white teeth, his dark wine-brown skin. I had felt so safe with him, a celibate lama.

Pajon looked at me. "There are some high lamas in the north," she said. "Kalsan lama is high. He is very learned and the abbot of a small monastery. He is a tulku, you know, a reincarnate lama. He used to be very high, then one of his nuns got pregnant and he married her. Now he is not quite as high as he was. He is still respected for his learning, though. He has studied as far as they go."

I remembered talking with him when he stopped in to visit Prema lama once, and his excitement about the idea of evolution and its convergence with Tibetan beliefs about human origins. He had a nice laugh. Pajon continued: "Some of the northern lamas are truly holy. There was one many years ago who came down from Tibet. He was a young man, an important tulku, and was traveling south with a small entourage. He was a very high lama and they carried him in a palanquin. The lama and his people stopped in Tebas at your father's house. He stayed in that little room you used to sleep in, above the courtyard. He had become ill on the journey and was very sick by the time they reached Tebas. He knew he was dying. He told his followers exactly when he would die and assumed a meditation position, sitting straight with his legs crossed. When the time arrived, he died but he stayed in that position for three days after death. Finally he fell over and they cremated his body. When they performed his funeral, lamas came from all around. It was a huge ceremony. You know the big stone resting platform below the village, the highest one? That was built as a memorial to him. He was a very high lama, skilled and powerful. He died so young, not even thirty years old. Come, it's late. Let's go to sleep."

She rolled out her bedding. I went outside and rinsed my face. The stars were cold and white and the village was quiet. Inside, Pajon lay covered with quilts, the lamp burning next to her. "Bolt the door, child," she said. I slid the wooden slat through the bolts. I sat for a moment on the mat and fingered my prayer beads as I whispered the mantras Maila lama had taught me, formulas for refuge and salutations to the bodhisattvas he had chosen for me. Then I climbed under the quilts. "Sleep now," said Pajon, and she blew out the lamp. The room was totally black. I could smell the acrid scent of the dead fire and hear Pajon's soft breathing. "Sleep well, Pajon," I said. "Mmm," she replied.

When I woke in the morning, the doors were open and the kettle sat on the fire. Anna's daughter Maya came in with a heavy water pot and shifted it up onto a platform near the door next to two others, wet and full. The morning sun glinted on their round copper sides illuminating the embossed designs on their curved bellies. Maya was silhouetted in the doorway, the light shining through a halo of hair strands loosed from her braid. "Still sleeping?" she asked me as I sat up. "I'm awake now," I replied. She turned and went down the steps. Pajon handed me a glass of tea and began to chop potatoes. I went out to the porch to wash my face. Mist rose over the village mingled with smoke from morning fires. A boy with a homespun shirt was taking a buffalo up the path to pasture, walking behind it with a long stick. It lumbered along the uneven stones, its broad body swaying, then paused and swung its head and snorted. The boy whacked it with the stick and they continued on.

After my face was clean, I shook out my lungi and retucked it, then wound the blue cotton sash around my waist to make a wide plump cummerbund. The cloth looked like a lake at my feet as I drew it up and wrapped it. It was snug around my middle, and the folds of the petticoat and lungi rustled against my legs as I walked. I reached to pick up the small brass water vessel, and the glass bangles on my arm jingled gently. I felt quiet inside on the still veranda, half hidden by shreds of mist. Sections of the gorge across from us showed in places where the mist was burning off, but the Himals remained veiled except for one small crown of a peak that jutted above the clouds.

Pajon and I were lingering in the courtyard after breakfast, combing our hair, when Apa arrived. The sun had burned through the fog and warmed the flagstones and we sat with our lungis pulled up and calves exposed. I tucked my legs up properly when he crossed the threshold. He was carrying a large khaki pack and smiling broadly.

"Look," he said, "One of our relations killed a deer. It doesn't happen much because they are protected. He gave half the meat to us to take back. Delicious venison. We'll be going soon, so get ready and come along." He sauntered off with the pack swung over his shoulder. I braided my hair and took up my bundle. Pajon was rolling up the mat. I carried it in for her and paused in the doorway.

"Go well," she said, "and come back soon."

"Stay well, Pajon," I replied. I bowed down to touch her feet and she took my hands. We looked into each other's eyes, then I slipped through the door and out of the courtyard.

The path went straight along to Ama's brother's house. The family had eaten and Ama was packing the last few items away for the walk back. The pack with the deer meat sat on the porch, pungent in the sun. Apa motioned to me.

"Take this, daughter," he said. I looked at the large pack skeptically. "Just for a ways," he continued, and handed it to me. I put it on.

We said good-bye to Grandmother, who bestowed her blessings, and to Mijou, her daughter-in-law, who bid us travel well. The young girl stood by her mother and saluted us as we left, her palms pressed together. Seyli and I walked behind Ama and Apa. As we walked, people in their court-yards called out: "Going so soon?" "Travel well." "Returning already?" Ama and Apa returned their brief greetings, not breaking the pace of the walk. Apa smiled and swung his walking stick, aluminum with a leather handle at the top, a gift from Hong Kong. I trudged along, glad I had wrapped the sash for the walk since it cushioned the weight of the pack against my back.

The sun was shining full force on the path beyond the village. *Charko* was the word to describe strong sun. The sound conveyed the meaning: harsh. Too much salt could also be *charko*: bitter, drying. Perspiration trickled down my back, soaking my blouse and gluing the pack to my body. It stank. The gorge widened a bit as we walked, and the angle of the terraced slopes softened.

"It's feeling heavy," I said to Apa.

"Let's stop and rest for a while," he said solicitously. There was a resting platform sheltered by a tree a little way ahead. The large flat stones were cool under the wide boughs of the tree. I slipped the pack off and felt the air against my damp back. It was nice. I had a drink from my water bottle. I could just see the edge of Cliff Shelter in the distance. We sat for a while. Ama had a cigarette.

"Let's go," said Apa. He handed me the pack. I felt dismayed and a little annoyed. I had already carried it for a couple of hours. "Just until Sohrya," he said, and held it while I slipped my arms through the straps. We continued on and I lagged behind, weighted by the venison. Seyli dawdled along with me. We approached Sohrya but Apa and Ama, ahead on the path, did not take the fork that led into the village but continued on the lower path, which skirted it. After another hour or two, we reached Tansen. The sky was a soft lavender streaked with pink. Ama and Apa waited for Seyli and me to catch up with them. "We won't reach Tebas before nightfall," said Apa. "We will spend the night with our relations here."

We spent the night with a middle-aged man and woman in their small house. I slept fitfully, huddled with Seyli on a mat on the floor. My body ached and I felt irritable. I woke early and washed my face, and after tea said I would go on ahead and and have breakfast at home. The path led through the jungle and I wanted some solitude. I liked the narrow waterfalls that trickled down the rocks, and the place where the path broke through the overhanging trees and skirted the ledge of a cliff, with tufts of grass poking out and the river far below. Looking down, I felt as though I were floating in space above the twisting river and patchwork fields. After only a few yards, the path reentered the jungle and soon reached the pool where village women bathed, then the stream where the water jugs were filled, then the village itself. It was an even path and a pleasant walk. I felt light and more cheerful as I thought of going home to Tson, alone and unburdened.

It was still early but the day promised to be warm. I gathered my bundle, rolling up the towel, change of clothes, toothbrush, and comb, and quickly rebraided my hair. I wished our host and hostess well and bowed to Ama and Apa. Apa rose and went over to the corner, picking up the khaki pack.

"Here, take this along," he said, holding it up for me to put on. I paused. Ama looked at me. The relatives sat quietly, watching. My breath was tight. I looked at the pack. It stank. It was stained on the back from yesterday's sweat. I felt everyone's eyes on me. I tightened my sash and looked out the door at the soft light on the flagstones. Then I slipped my arms through the straps, turned, and strode out.

Tears stung my eyes as I walked. I went quickly, staring at the path ahead. The trail sloped up toward the jungle and the pack felt heavy. The sun was stronger in the open beyond the village and I felt the sweat begin to prickle at my neck. The pack was pulling on my shoulders and I leaned forward to bear the weight more solidly on my back. The way through the jungle was cooler but my blouse was soaked and the bloody scent of the venison was overwhelming. I pushed down the feeling of nausea and walked faster.

Kanchi was rocking the baby on the porch when I entered the court-yard, pulling a rope that was tied to the basket that cradled him, air waft-ing the covering cloth that protected Ratna from light and flies. Tson was cooking by the fire.

"You've come," she said.

"I've come," I replied.

"What's that?" she asked.

"It's Apa's horrible stinking deer meat!" I said, flinging the pack on the floor. I burst into tears. "He made me carry it all the way from Torr. 'Only a little ways,' he said." Maila looked up, startled, from a corner. I grabbed my bundle. "I'm going to Cliff Shelter," I said, "where people don't treat me like that."

"Don't you want some food first?" asked Tson.

"No," I replied. "I don't want anything."

Kanchi looked up curiously as I stormed out of the courtyard and down the path. I kept my eyes down and walked quickly, past the bamboo grove and out of the village. I pounded down the mountain, not resting at any of the shady platforms, stamping my rage out on the stone steps that wound zigzagging to the river below. When I got to the bottom I felt wobbly and faint, still teary but more sulky than enraged. I slipped past the shop at Dusam, not wanting to face Amrit Kumari. I could imagine her probing questions, teasing, and acerbic remarks. Continuing, I forded the river and saw a lone, long Thakali house by the river, where they served tea and snacks to travelers. I did not know them well and could have some food in peace, I thought. I was starving.

They had tables outside and the shallow water bubbled pleasantly across the rocks in front of their house. The two pretty daughters, resting after breakfast, came to sit with me while I ate and their mother joined us after a while. I resisted their intrusion into my sulky solitude, but warmed to their company as they joked and laughed.

"You have no companion," they said. "Time to find a husband. Are those gold bracelets part of your marriage gift? A good husband will give you something really big and delicious (gales of laughter). Marry our brother and come live here."

"But you'll go off and leave me with your mother, who'll work me till I drop, while you enjoy your husbands' tasty things," I replied. We laughed until the tears rolled down our cheeks.

Their father, an elderly shaman, walked by as we giggled and looked at us sternly. "Have you women no work?" he asked.

I stood to go and paid for my meal. "Not the tea," said the mother, returning a rupee note. The gentleness of the land around the river was soothing. I forded it again a little further on, then the path rose. The sun was warm and I could hear the gurgling, sparkling river below, growing fainter as I proceeded higher. The path was broad and smooth as it inclined into the woods, where it levelled off again, and the light through the leaves made mottled patterns on the ground. As the trees thinned and the woods opened, I could hear the soft roar of the waterfall at the entrance to Cliff Shelter. There was a gash in the slope where a landslide had carried off a chunk of of the hillside and I picked my way across it stepping on the flattened footsteps of those who had crossed before, making little ledges on the slope. Then the path resumed and I could see the swirling pool beneath the wide waterfall on the other side of the river. The pouring, gleaming water looked tranquil as it tumbled down the rocks, as though the motion was stilled in its constancy. Fallen water moved across the pool, smooth and stately, and joined the flowing river.

I could see the edges of the houses at the top of the bazaar. The first one belonged to Bhimsen's youngest brother. It was tall and narrow, colored with red clay. His daughters, chatting on the porch, greeted me as I walked by. A little further down was the small square house of the bangle seller, festoons of colored bangles displayed on the wall, along with ribbons, hairpins, and little combs. Some bottles of red nail polish sat on a shelf against the wall. It was getting to be midday and the sun shone down on the white stone street of the bazaar. I passed the post office, with its large wooden signboard showing the two red triangles of the Nepali flag. Down a few steps was the temple and behind it a bit of the river was showing, shallow and bubbly. The village became flat here, the river lapping at the sand and stones behind the houses, where women washed their clothes. The tailor shop was across from the temple, a small shabby house with a sewing machine on the porch. Bhimsen's sister lived a few doors down from that. Her husband had recently died of cancer, and I thought he had been resurrected when I saw his twin brother in the street on the day of the funeral. She seemed so young to be alone.

As I approached Bhimsen's place, the broad street narrowed. In the house before his a Gurung family lived, a young retired soldier who had led his Gurkha regiment's marching band and his wife, two children, and the wife's elderly mother. Since his wife was an only child, he had come to live in her home, a position considered degrading to the male but happy for the woman, who remained in her own home, secure and powerful. He did not seem to mind, and was kind to his family, bantering playfully with his wife and joking with passersby as he sat in the doorway under a picture of himself stepping out with the military band, Queen Elizabeth standing benignly nearby. They were an outspoken and cheerful family. Days before as she sat on a mat in the sun, the old woman had instructed me to tell God that she wanted to die before she was drooling in her food and peeing in her clothes, saying "Too long a life is not a good thing, child. Tell him I'll be ready to go at about sixty-five." I greeted her as I walked by.

Bhimsen had two tall houses that towered over a narrow section of the street, casting shadows across the pavement except at midday. Now the porch across from the kitchen, on the further side of the street, was bathed in sunlight. There were two long wooden tables there with benches on either side. Two tourists sat at one table drinking tea and Bhimsen sat at the other. His daughter sat on the doorstep of the kitchen peeling potatoes. Manju looked up and smiled, "O sister," she said.

"You've come," said Bhimsen. "Put your things down and sit. Manju, get her some tea." The tourists glanced over. I could hear the river babbling in the background. A few flies buzzed around. It was very peaceful. I felt happy, like a well cared-for child. "You have returned quickly," said

Bhimsen. It was usually a couple of weeks between visits. "Yes," I replied. The cliffs on the other side of the river rose high over the bazaar, shadowed and craggy. I wondered what to say. Manju put a glass of tea in front of me. "I got angry and left," I said.

"What happened?"

"Apa made me carry a big pack of venison all the way from Torr to Tebas." I felt embarrassed. It seemed so petty. "He said I would just need to carry it to Sorhya. He kept giving it back when I thought I was done. It was heavy and smelly, and I felt really mad by the time I got home, so I left the pack and came here."

"Did you say you were coming?"

"I told Tson. Ama and Apa were not back yet."

"Rest tonight and go back tomorrow," Bhimsen said. "Don't stay away too long. Manju, give her some potatoes." He rose and paced up the street slowly, his hands behind his back. He had been in the military for many years and stood erect, surveying the bazaar as though it were a parade ground, checking it approvingly.

The tourists looked at me with curiosity but I did not feel like talking with them. I slipped into the kitchen after Manju and sat on a mat with her and her mother. A pan of potatoes sat by the fire and Manju spooned some into a dish for me. "Eat," she said, "we had some before."

"You've come back soon," said her mother.

"She got mad," Manju said. "Jimwal made her carry a big load from Torr and she was fed up and came here."

"Mm," said her mother. She continued to grind spices. I ate my potatoes. The kitchen was peaceful, small but with a large window as well as a door. I could see the great house of Bhimsen's elder brother. The lower floor was a shop. He had never been a soldier, but stayed home and traded, running mule trains, selling from the shop. He had six daughters but no son. Four daughters were in Cliff Shelter, two more in Horse Water with his first wife, three days further north. He seemed skeptical of me and completely ignored me when I was present. I did not mind, as that was reasonable behavior toward a young female. His daughters were warm and boisterously affectionate. I could see the eldest one tending the shop, laughing with a village woman.

I felt lonely and at loose ends, embarrassed with my empty plate there in front of me. Who did I think I was, running off in a fit of pique? Manju's mother's back was rounded away from me as she ground the cumin seeds, her weight pressed into the pestle, long thick braid laced with gray. Did I deserve the kindness of these people? Manju glanced at me.

"Are you going to take a bath?" she asked.

I stirred from my thoughts and looked out at the river, silver ripples from the sun, flecks of foam where the current hit a rock, dark green and light green, roaring where the two rivers met, one from the north, one from the east, clear clean water, swirling, tumbling, singing. "A bath?"

"You've walked so far in the heat," she said. "A bath might refresh you. Then I'll be done with my work for a while and we can go to the shop and visit my cousins." She smiled and picked up my plate, touching my knee.

I had a small towel and a change of clothes in my bundle, and Manju's mother gave me a brass pot for dipping the water. Children came to watch but I didn't mind. I had become adept at modest bathing, pulling my petticoat up above my breasts so I was covered from there to my knees as I washed myself inside the cloth. Women who had come to wash their clothes greeted me and chatted. I did feel refreshed. The cool water and easy company pulled me back to the world from my thoughts and worries.

I slept well that night. The darkness amplified the river sounds, the current pulling me under, out of consciousness, as I lay on the small wooden cot in the wide wooden room upstairs above the street. It was like lying on a platform inside an ark, water all around. In the morning before the first slivers of dawn came through the shutters, I could hear the mule bells chime, faintly and then louder, punctuated by the clopping of the mules' hoofs. I lay and listened. "Manju . . . Manjoo," her mother called out. The animals jostled as they passed under the house where the street narrowed. "Hoy, get on," cried the mule driver as his stick thwacked a mule's back. First the clopping, then the bells faded in the morning air. Waterpots clanged below. Opening the shutter above the bed, I saw Manju going toward the river with a large jug. I brushed my hair and braided a ribbon into it. I could see the red glow of the kitchen fire, and the houses and trees taking shape in the pale light. The rock outcroppings of the cliff stood out against the sky. I picked my way carefully down the dim stairs and sat at the table on the veranda. Manju's mother brought me some tea. Bhimsen joined me at the table. "You're up."

"I'm up," I replied. "I'll go back today."

"After breakfast?" he inquired.

"Before, I think," I answered.

"Mm," he said, "Good. The climb gets harder in the heat. The headman's family will be waiting for you."

"Mm," I said, looking at my tea.

"You'll be down again soon to check your mail, I expect," he said.

"Yes, in not too long," I said. "It is always nice to stay." I finished my tea. "I should pay my bill and go."

"Not this time, child," he said. "You stayed just a little while."

"Even so," I protested, "I ate and slept."

"Even so," he said. "I won't take your money."

Tears came to my eyes. "Stay well, Father."

"Go well, child."

The bangle shop was still shuttered when I passed it and the path through the woods above Cliff Shelter was damp with morning dew. I balanced across the logs that criss-crossed the river at its low point and walked along the riverbank. The morning air was fresh and a light mist hung in patches, veiling sections of the path. I walked out of the mist as the path rose. The trail became rocky as I reached the great stone staircase winding up to the village. Nothing was visible but the vast mountainside carved with terraces. Little cornstalks were beginning to grow in the dry fields. I looked back at the mist lying in the valley and thought of how the huge soft monsoon clouds would roll up the gorge from the south in a few weeks and the fields and paths would run with water. The stones were dusty as I walked. I sat under the tree at a resting place about halfway up the path. High above me, the prayer flags flapped at the edge of the village on tall knotted bamboo poles, their edges shredded by the wind. Some roofs jutted out behind them. I felt tired. I swung my legs as I sat, stretched them, thought of going on, waited a bit longer. A haze of smoke hovered over the village, morning cooking fires. I thought of Tson and Ama clearing up the tea things and preparing the morning meal. Apa would likely be in the courtyard weaving long, thin strips of bamboo into baskets, the radio on beside him. The morning program of old Indian film tunes was his favorite. I swung my legs a bit longer. A buffalo lumbered down the path, followed by two eight-or nine-year-old boys. "Hey, it's the white-woman," one of them said. I stood up and took my bundle.

"Where are you coming from," he asked.

"Down below," I said. "I went to Cliff Shelter and came back. Where are you off to?"

"Taking the buffalo out to graze," the boy answered, whacking it on the flank with a stick and continuing on.

After the path curves away from the cliff edge and goes past the bamboo grove (where women flutter their shawls to scare away lingering ghosts), the stone steps thrust straight up the center of the village, walls and court-yards on either side. An old woman sitting in the sun called to me, "O child. Where are you coming from?"

"Down below, Grandmother. I've been to Cliff Shelter."

I reached the gate of our courtyard and hesitated. I could see Apa, the bald patch on his head shiny in the morning light, his t-shirt hanging loose over his shoulders. Kanchi sat beside him chatting as he worked. "O Apa," I said. He turned to me and I pressed my hands together and bowed.

"You've come," he said.

"I've come."

"Have you eaten?"

"Not yet," I said.

"Then go in the house." He turned back to his weaving. Kanchi looked at me then continued her conversation.

Tson sat by the fire finishing her meal and Ama lay relaxing on the cot near the hearth, smoking a cigarette. "O Ernestine," she said. "You've come." Tson looked at me.

"I've come."

"Have you eaten?" Tson asked.

I stood in the center of the room holding my bundle. Smoke drifted up from the embers of the fire and wafted through the door. I looked at the floor. The clay was smooth, still damp in places. I felt like a stranger. I thought I might cry. "Not yet," I replied.

"Put your bundle down and eat something," Ama said.

After I finished my meal, Tson took the dishes out to wash them.

"Come here and sit," Ama said, motioning me to the edge of the cot. She sat up and looked into my face. "This is not at all like your country, is it?"

"No," I replied, "not at all."

"Apa was hurt and upset that you got angry and ran off to Cliff Shelter. He thought, 'Isn't she willing to carry even a little bundle?' "

"Not *so* little," I said softly.

"Even so," Ama continued. "I think I understand what happened. You felt like he tricked you, like he didn't keep his promises."

I nodded.

"Well, there is a lot you don't understand. It doesn't look so good for an important man like your father to carry a pack while a big daughter walks along free. It looks good for a daughter to help. Now no one wants to carry a big pack of stinky deer meat." She drew on her cigarette and smiled. "It's heavy and you walk along with that stinky smell in your nose." I smiled. "From the time our children are small, we coax them. We might say, 'Now Seyli, just carry this as far as the resting place.' So she agrees and picks it up. But at the resting place we say, 'Just a little farther,' like that, on and on, until we are home. If we said, 'Carry it all the way,' she would refuse. So we coax her to do it, little by little. Children here know from the time they are young that it's all a fake; they make all kinds of excuses not to pick up a pack because they know they won't get to put it down again. Now Apa was just treating you like a real daughter, but you couldn't understand that because people don't do it that way in your country."

I looked at her sitting there in the dim room with her glowing cigarette, tobacco leaves poking out the unlit end, strands of hair loose around her face, her eyes kind and serious. She had wrapped her mind around my world and had understood it. She had seen the gap: this is what I got; this is where I missed; this is why I had behaved badly. She had been able to compare her world to mine and find the emotional slippage, and with her explanation she created a platform for me to stand on and see the differences. "That's right," I said. "It was just like that."

Tson had returned toward the end of the conversation. "We thought you just did not want to work," she said, "that you didn't like to carry a heavy pack."

"But I work around the village," I protested.

"She did not understand because her country is different," said Ama. "Let's go outside and braid our hair."

- Urban vs. rural life
- Buddhist nun - relationship w/
  4 created self as something diff.
- Anthropologist cannot escape
  from their history.

6.

Creating Selves, Crafting Lives

In a world where place and power were clearly mapped, I was peculiar. My attributes tugged in different directions. I was young and female, powerless by definition. A young female belongs to the lineage. She is a potential gift to another family, a link between lineages and clans, a vehicle for their continuity, producing from her body generations of those clan members. Grown, she can whisper to her girl-child, "You are a Plun woman's daughter," calling up the root of her own clan. The girl herself will go forth as a daughter of her father's clan, a thread cast out to weave the clans together, perpetuating their symmetry. But I was no one's gift. A Plun woman's daughter through love and fiction, I could not be given. I was not really of my father's clan, though adoption placed me in his matrix of kinship: this one's sister; that one's niece. But I had been drawn into their world through the affection, interest, amusement of women. I was born of their imagination. The men did not own me, and could only claim me loosely. They could not command me.

On my way back from Pokhara once, I stayed the night in an inn run by friends in Nine Hills. Some Gurkha soldiers were staying there, and as usual when speaking Nepali, I referred to the place I lived as "our village" and to Ama and Apa as "my parents." A large middle-aged man looked at my lungi and Gurung shawl, my red glass bangles and ribboned braid, the attire the women had insisted on for me and taught me to wear, and told me it was wrong, and I was wrong, and that what I was engaging in was a masquerade to which I had no right. I was not going to stay there. I was not going to marry there. I was not going to suffer there. I was not a Gurung and to call these people my parents was a pretense. Hollow.

Ridiculous. Wrong. I realized the truth of his words and shrunk back into myself. I had come freely and I would go freely. My only obligations were the ones I chose. I did not belong. I cried myself to sleep and walked somberly back to the village. I told Ama what he had said. "Oh Ernestine," she said. "If your parents scold you, you should cry. If some stranger scolds you, don't even listen." Restored to my tenuous place (perhaps all things defined by women are tenuous), I went on.

The place that women gave me was the present, time and space intertwined, concrete and immediate, but I carried with me in my person a history. I was white. I was from a wealthy and powerful country. I was educated. This tugged against the subordination of my youth and femininity rendering me strange, a walking paradox. The history was more a symbolic overtone, though, the echo of another world. The exclamations when I entered the village had been physical: "so thin"; "so young"; "barely grown up." The response to my presence had been to protect and instruct, but also to hope that some American wealth would stay and that the prestige of the bullying powerful West would bring honor to the household that sheltered me. What if I had been low caste and poor?

Women like that had come there. A woman referred to as Tiger's mother, because her two little boys had been nicknamed Tiger and Jackal, had arrived in the village destitute. Her husband had gambled away their little bit of land and then had died from drink. She was strong and willing, and helped in our household and several others. For this she got a room and food for her family. They were given old clothes and occasional gifts of new ones, sometimes a little money. She invested this in chickens and sold their eggs, and she made home-brewed liquor and sold it to the men. She claimed her lower (but not untouchable) caste was really the same as the middle-level caste of a people who lived in nearby villages. She changed her name and then married her lithe and pretty daughter into a family in one of those villages, but the daughter resented the marriage and returned, resisting the coaxings of her young husband and the pressure of her mother and the village elders. She had to serve them and work in the fields, she said. She hated it. A town life with evenings at the cinema was more what she had in mind, or at least a soldier husband, with trips to India and a few pretty and fashionable things. After the marriage dissolved, she became the housekeeper for Prema lama in his new house (red windows and a balcony) to the astonishment and shock of the neighbors. They disapproved, but her mother was not blamed. "A willful girl," they said, "shameless." "What kind of lama is that," they said, "living with a woman." The boys were well behaved, though the little one was sickly. He had a sweet face, round and pale with runny eyes.

Tiger's mother was absorbed as a servant, not adopted. She was a member of the village, addressed respectfully with kinship terms, but only the more generic ones, and usually just by children. No one called her "dharma daughter" or made her a ritual friend, categories that offer the full status of a relative. Her daughter longed for what most young women wished, but it was so far out of reach that the only way she could come close to it was by going completely beyond the pale of respectability. Not like my sisters, offering tea in rooms above the bazaar in china cups brought back from Hong Kong. From the balcony, we looked down on the curved tops of taxis, the red ceremonial umbrellas of marriage processions, the headdresses and crowns of the men possessed by the goddess Durga as they danced the length of the street. Carts, muletrains, horses, trucks and smoky buses, beggars without legs, men doing business, boys on bicycles, village girls giggling in their shawls, the pretty prostitutes who sang and danced in local clubs, mad dogs: we could watch them all go by. Once you had been to the town how could you forget it, so full of life and motion? In comparison, the steep mountains of the village seemed dull and barren. "Oh look," someone would say, "a man going up the path across the gorge with a buffalo." On a truly exciting day the bangle seller or cloth merchant might show up. To young people like her it felt confined and stifling, especially with no status to maintain and no wealth. She lived with the lama for a while, then she drifted off, no one knew for certain where.

Eventually the lama left, too. It turned out that Pajon was right. The villagers did not like him. First there was an incident at a funeral, where some young men got drunk and told him his presence was not welcome in the village. I was told there was a scuffle, quickly broken up. For a few days the lama stayed mainly around the household of his ritual friend. The two men of the house had been away for months in the army with their families. Prema was the ritual friend of the eldest brother. Their house was on the terrace below ours, reached by climbing down a series of stone wedges set in the wall supporting the terrace. The climber then descended into a tall narrow passage between two gray stone walls that emerged next to the buffalo stall. It smelled of hay and dung and opened out on a view of the gorge winding north. Our sister, the headman's second daughter, had married the younger son, a soldier in the British army and they had been in Hong Kong for several years. The mother would occasionally bring gifts of milk or curds, apologetic that her son, from a simple family, had made off with such a prestigious bride. The old woman was constantly working, though in her seventies. "When I cannot do this any longer, they can throw me on the cremation fire," she said. It was as though she were keeping death at bay. She could have hired laborers to help but she chopped and hauled her own firewood, planted the crops and harvested them, processed the grain for storage, wove cloth for carrying bags. Her house was small, but there was a spacious and airy room off to the side where the lama lived. He called her mother, teased her, complimented her good cooking, and came home with interesting stories from his trips to other villages and the town. She made him tasty delicacies and placed a thick blanket on the mat when she served his dinner. When he heard her sons were to return, he began to build his house.

Prema lama's father had been a Thakali lama from the north. He was a married lama with a Thakali wife and family. Prema's mother was a Gurung woman from a village about a day's walk from Tebas. She had a liaison with the father, but he did not stay with her nor did he have a great deal to do with his son. When he was still a little boy, maybe eight or nine, Prema was sent to be a monk at the monastery. He learned Tibetan, Buddhist philosophy, a little medicine, ritual procedures, and then in his late teens, he left. He earned some money assisting at rituals, but he was neither here nor there. He was a northern lama, but not quite a northerner. He was certainly not a village-based Gurung lama. He spoke Gurung and lived in Gurung villages, but belonged to no Gurung clan. His Gurung mother was a distant figure whom he seldom saw. His Thakali father was dead and the "senior mother," his father's wife, acknowledged but did not welcome him. He looked Thakali—tall and lean—and spoke Thakali but had no home among Thakalis. He was handsome and clearly liked women, but to marry would diminish his status and rob him of the freedom to roam and cultivate opportunities. He had no inheritance with which to build the life of a householder. He was intelligent, but not among the most learned lamas nor the most spiritually advanced. If he had spiritual aspirations, they were not evident. He was fluid, slipping across boundaries, shaping himself to fit chances that he encountered. Here he got goods from Hong Kong and sold them at a profit. There he bought some gold to wear with his fine, well-draped maroon robes. He chanted in ceremonies, long fingers turning the leaves of the sacred books, shoulder to shoulder with the high lamas from the north, his learning placing him above the Gurung lamas in the line of officiants. He moved from his ritual friend's airy room to his own house where the pretty girl cooked for him, and later he left for the town, pressed out by low-key hostility. I ran into him in the bazaar one day and he opened the door to his place there and showed it to me: a smallish room, dim, with a chest in the corner, a wooden cot, and red and yellow curtains. "It needs a woman's touch," he said, and smiled.

The bazaar is the refuge of misfits. People are not defined by their roots there; they create themselves anew. People are drawn by the comforts and amenities. "I can send my child to school," they would say. "There is medicine if we get sick." "Not such unending hard toil as in the village." But there was also an edge, the excitement of possibility. A person could live on his own terms. The two village houses constructed according to Prema's plan were suspect. All the others had one open space and an attic, windows covered with latticed screens. His windows opened boldly, sporting red shutters. Within were rooms, secret spaces, the house not open to view. What might be hidden there? What goings on might be possible? Then there was the indecorous touch in his own house of the balcony, where one could overlook the mountains and peer down on the neighbors. People did not like it. The house was an affront to Gurung values, an intrusion, just as he was an intrusion, presuming on their graciousness. It was built at a diagonal off the main path, throwing the regularity of the village askew.

In Pokhara bazaar, a person could have any kind of house. I heard no critical house commentaries there. Prema had introduced me to the bazaar. Tourists stayed in hotels, which were down by the lake or near the airport. I had stayed in one briefly on the way to the village. The bazaar was one long, winding street of shops and houses. It seemed to admit no foreigners, except those who might work at the college or hospital and have their own houses. It seemed closed, not porous, with its own life and direction, not turned outward like the lakeside hotels. I was going to town for some medicine and he said to me, "Stay with my friends. They give food and lodging for a few rupees a day." I found the household he described. The woman was brisk and unfriendly. "It's all one room," she said. "I can't give you anything special." All the inns I stayed in were all one room. I told her I didn't mind. "Men stay here, too," she said. "Aren't you ashamed?" She looked me up and down. I did not, at that time, understand the connection of shame to social propriety and took the question literally. "No, I am not ashamed," I replied. She snorted. After a couple of visits filled with shouting and snorting (I was not the only object of her derision) she told me that though I might not mind (snort) it damaged their reputation to keep men and women in the same room. People would talk. I should find somewhere else to stay. I felt disappointed to think of leaving the aliveness of the bazaar for the scenic beauty and tourist wonders of the lake. I did not want to live in a postcard, even for a few days. This was before either of my sisters had moved to the bazaar.

Prema closed his eyes and thought, then sent me to other friends. These were a young woman whose mother owned the inn I stayed in at Fort of the Moon and whose husband was from Cliff Shelter. She charged a bit more, but was vivacious and funny. I knew her mother and sister well and felt quite at home with her, which took the edge off the loneliness of being away from the village. She was very pretty, with four children, whom she said were her high school diploma, B.A., M.A., and Ph.D. Once I was lying on a bed in her house reading, and I looked up to see her standing in the doorway, with tears streaming down her face. "Elder sister," I cried, "what's wrong?"

"I see you looking and looking, and imagine all the things you see in your books. I can never know them. I cannot read at all. Like a blind person, I can never know the things you see." She wiped her eyes. I thought of how she insisted her eldest daughter attend to her studies, not just the sons. The daughter was a bright and serious girl, who did well in school. The mother spoke five languages—Thakali, Tibetan, Gurung, Newari, and Nepali—but there had been no schools when she was growing up. I had never valued my books and their secrets so much; the weight of the book and the smoothness of its cover in my hands felt like a treasure. I told my daughter about it when she went to school.

"Not everyone gets to know these things."

"But why did she cry?"

"Because she thought there were such wonderful things in the books and she would never get to know them."

"Didn't you teach her?"

"No. But her children learned to read. They can read like you do now." She dried her eyes and we stood at the window looking out. Some women were buying cloth at the shop across the way. It was a tall house on the main street of the bazaar. The other one in which I had stayed had been at the edge of town, more rustic, with a corn field next door and the guest room on the ground floor. Here I slept up high. She liked me and put me in a small room by the family quarters. Below us was a larger guest room. One night it was rowdy with noise and music; young men come to the country from Kathmandu, drinking and looking for prostitutes. The sound came up through the floor and I lay in bed and looked through the shutters at the night sky, waiting for their revels to end. She told me excitedly the next day that she had peeked in and seen girls dancing for them, "showing everything you can think of." The husband told them to leave the next day and said they weren't having men from the city any more. He was a businessman and as the family prospered they took fewer paying guests and moved to a bigger house away from the main street. The new house was cement and had a garden in the back.

I felt like no one in the town. Divorced from the known, not mapped by the coordinates of kinship, I felt lost. I was friendly with my hostess. We chatted and shared confidences and joked with her clever and kindly husband, but the basis of our relationship was clear. Always there was the little something she wanted to sell me: a sari that would look just right, a nice little purse. I was usually in town for medical treatment, this dysentery, that intractable fever. This made the place seem all the more lonely and tiresome. My hostess's warmth, good humor, and nice cooking made my stay pleasant, but it never felt like home. I floated, uncreated, ghostly, as all the sights of the bazaar whirled past. Too many possibilities, too little solid ground.

My refuge was Dharmamitra. I had discovered her when I returned from the meditation retreat in India and came to the Pokhara bazaar for the first time on my way to the village. Someone had told me there was a Theravada temple in the town, the same school of Buddhism that I had studied. I had been so moved and cleansed by those days of pain and silence, I wanted to find a touchstone to return to. Yes, the people in town told me, there was a Buddha *vihar*. It was down some streets behind the cinema. These weren't the streets the taxis traversed, straight and bustling. They curved. They meandered like streams of a river, running through stands of banana trees, bougainvillea, ferns and fronds of various kinds. They were lush and quiet. Small brick houses stood here and there. There were a few large, walled compounds with great houses set in the middle. It was a Newar neighborhood, old and established, with dwellings large enough to house extended families and ancillary houses for servants and poor people. Little girls with braids walked here and there, bringing water in large brass jugs. A well-kept cow or two wandered down the road. I could barely speak Nepali at that point. "Buddha Vihar?" I said to a medium-sized child. She looked at me solemnly and pointed down a nearby street. I proceeded.

Opposite a large compound was a wall with a great arched entrance, like the gateway to an arcade. Across the top in Nepali script was written "Buddha Vihar." I walked through it. Around me were fruit trees and flowering beds. I looked up at the top windows of a small brick house. The front door was open, but I hesitated to enter. As I stood there, a woman in orange robes appeared at the door. She greeted me with palms pressed together. I returned the greeting. She beckoned me to enter. The ground floor was a windowless storage area with stairs leading up to the second floor. This was a large open room with windows all around that let in the warm afternoon light. A small golden dog with long hair approached and sniffed my feet. In back I could see a luxuriant vegetable garden and a cow tethered under a thatched shelter. The square, open room contrasted with the expansive, unrestrained life of the garden. It was spare and simple, all lines and right angles. There was a bed in the corner, a rectangular carpet next to it, and in the center of the room was a table with flowers. It was in front of a large plaster Buddha, white with yellow robes, backed with a halo of colored Christmas-tree lights. I bowed formally before it, placing my head on the floor. Dharmamitra motioned me to sit on one of the mats against the wall. I smiled and sat. She took a few steps up a ladder and said something in rapid Newari to someone on the third floor. She asked me a question in Nepali that contained words like "drink" and "tea." I got the general idea but could not work out how to phrase the answer. I smiled and nodded, twisting the edge of my blouse. A woman in a sari came down the ladder with two cups of tea on a tray. Dharmamitra handed me one. I smiled. It was milky and delicious. The woman went back up the ladder.

"Tasty," I said in Nepali. She smiled.

"My name is Dharmamitra," she said slowly, enunciating each word carefully. I got it. It was one of the phrases that came in early in my language text. I began to feel adventurous.

"My name is Ernestine." I shaped each word attentively with my tongue, feeling the excitement of being entirely on my own, having a real conversation. "I come from America."

She smiled. "Good," she said. We sat together for some time, drinking and having shreds of conversation. In the silences, I looked at the walls. Pictures of the king and queen of Nepal hung on the wall behind the Buddha. There was a portrait of the Buddha's mother, Queen Maya, sleeping against a dark blue background and dreaming of the elephant that would announce the Buddha's birth, touching her stomach with a lotus. It looked at her tenderly. On another wall was a calendar showing the life cycle, like an accelerated action photo, with a woman in a swimsuit whose body withered with age through each successive frame until she was wrinkled and bent: an icon of impermanence. Beneath it were the clean, clear lines of the days and weeks. I finished my tea.

She walked me to the door. Near the doorway was a framed black-and-white picture of the queen of Nepal handing Dharmamitra a certificate. They stood in front of some long, low buildings. Dharmamitra's shaved head was inclined and the queen stood erect, with dark glasses and a bouffant hairdo, a sweater over her sari. "Her Majesty," said Dharmamitra when she saw me peering at the photo. I learned later that Dharmamitra had started the first girls' high school in the area and the queen had come to cut the ribbon. Dharmamitra walked me to the gate. We bowed to each other under the archway. Evening was beginning to fall as I strolled down the winding street. When I looked back, I could see the garland of little lights around the Buddha twinkling through the window.

As she created the girls' school, a fine thing of great integrity, Dharmamitra had invented herself. I loved the little compound with the garden and the vihar, the young cow lowing in the back, and I went there frequently whenever I was in town. As my language improved, our conversations became more intimate and our visits less formal. She always gave me tea and began to include rich and delicious snacks as part of the hospitality, with little tidbits on a plate to the side for her dog, Silk. The walled house across the street, large and imposing, was the home in which she had been born and grown up. Her family still lived there.

Her nephew was a teacher and came almost daily with his best friend to see her. They talked religion and politics and played cards. When she lost, Dharmamitra would slam her cards down with a flourish and shout "Rascal!" at the winner, and they would all laugh. I usually watched as the only card games I knew were Go Fish and War. They tried to teach me Rummy once, but I was very slow and tended to be overly deferential which made the game very boring, so I was relegated to my position as observer. I sat by the window across from the plaster Buddha, fortified with tea and snacks, enjoying their play or feeling bored and stroking Silk, watching the road for visitors. When visitors approached, for devotions or to seek advice, the card players would collect the deck and tuck the small red box behind a picture frame. Any lit cigarettes would quickly be stubbed out. Dharmamitra would stand and smooth her robes and the nephew and friend would leave or fade into a corner. Sometimes it was a woman from a village to make offerings, sometimes a town dweller seeking advice about a quarrel in the family, sometimes an old man come to discuss political conditions.

Nepal strongly proclaimed itself a Hindu kingdom, tolerant of other religions but Hindu in identity. From a Hindu perspective, the king himself was a deity. The Theravada Buddhism practiced at the vihar was new to Nepal. It had come as part of an international social reform movement started by a Buddhist leader called Dharmapala in Sri Lanka. It was spread by Buddhist missionaries. Theravada in Nepal retained an international flavor. Dharmamitra was visited by monks from Thailand and Sri Lanka, by nuns from Japan.

In her lifetime, Nepal had gone from a country closed to foreigners to one teeming with tourists and various foreign aid workers. It had emerged from over a century of crushing domination by the harsh and repressive Rana family, who had intermarried with the royal family (the king as deity could not be completely displaced) but not allowed them to rule, and now had a more fluid government wherein the king did actually rule. In the early 1950s, after India had ejected the British colonialists, the Nepalese too rose up against the brutality of their leaders, removed the Ranas and restored their king to power. Early in the new regime, under King Tribhuvan, democracy flourished. Dharmamitra had participated in the uprising against the Ranas and had friends among the leaders who became part of the new democratic government. It was a heady time, filled with the exhilaration of freedom and hope. There was free speech and popular representation, but after a decade King Mahendra, Tribhuvan's son, asserted that Nepal was not ready for "Western-style" democracy and forbade the freedoms that had taken root, jailing large numbers of the opposition, and placing all authority in his own person. People said his idealistic father would have wept.

From the early 1960s until the People's Revolution in 1990, Nepal was an absolute monarchy. There were some elected representatives, but they had only advisory power. At the time I lived in Nepal, censorship was complete and resistance to the government could be expressed only obliquely. The rhetoric of Hinduism was powerful, supporting the king's unquestioned authority. The newspaper was full of large photos of the royal family receiving dignitaries and doing good deeds. News of opposition leaders imprisoned or exiled, radical students who disappeared, the questionable activities of people of influence did not make the press. People talked quietly of misdeeds and atrocities. There were moments of resistance: an all-day strike, a march "celebrating" an ethnic festival that everyone knew to be a way of showing strength and opposition, a boycott of the government dairy when the grapevine made it known that bribed officials had bought powdered milk that came from cows contaminated by the blast in Chernobyl (some "agitators" were arrested, the newspaper reported, for reviling His Majesty's milk, and milk from all other sources, including baby formula, was taken out of the market). The king was shown going to the great Hindu temples, like Ram (another incarnation of Vishnu), the paradigm of the righteous and just ruler, protector of the people. To be non-Hindu was to be outside the locus of power.

The Theravada community in Kathmandu, though only a few dacades old, was large. Contrasting with traditional Tantric Buddhism in its more rational and pragmatic approach, it attracted intellectuals and large numbers of merchant and professional families: the rising bourgeoisie. These were neither by class nor caste the king's constituency. I got to know some of the nuns from Kathmandu through Dharmamitra. More formal than Dharmamitra, they were nonetheless kind to me when I was in the city, taking me to the monastery to converse with learned monks and showing me around the nunneries in the Kathmandu valley. This was a much more organized world than that of the Pokhara community.

One kind and friendly nun, Tini, brought me to a ceremony where a statue donated by the Thai ambassador was being unveiled. Hundreds of people were there and the upper end of the hall was filled with lines of saffron-robed monks and nuns. Five-colored Buddhist banners hung from the building. Aromas of the feast to follow wafted through the afternoon air. The Theravadan constituency in Kathmandu was almost entirely made up of one caste: Buddhist Newars whose rich Tantric rituals were now supplemented with this imported modern version of their faith. There was ceremonial Pali chanting and there were speeches, most in the Newari language, during which time I sat and enjoyed the warm sun, happily anticipated the feast, and understood not a word. I noticed that many sari-clad, bejeweled women around me were also glancing about and chatting, fluency in Newari notwithstanding, as the earnest speakers went on and on. Finally, a distinguished man stood up to thank the Thai delegation for their gift. Speaking in English, he thanked them with elaborate and ornate words and then said quite plainly, "This is a Hindu kingdom in which our religion exists under threat. Without the involvement of the international Buddhist community, we would not be allowed to survive. Please do not forget us." The crowd applauded long and loudly. The Thai ambassador then graciously acknowledged their thanks. After this, the assembled company filed past the great line of monks and nuns, seated in order of precedence: the monks senior to junior and the nuns below them. Offerings were made. Then great vats of food were uncovered. Monks, nuns, and dignitaries were served and then the assembly lined up, heaped their plates and ate, the huge courtyard filled well into the afternoon with seated circles of family and friends flung out like hoops in the sun.

In Pokhara, Dharmamitra was alone. Nuns from Kathmandu visited on occasion, but she was a one-woman organization, defining her role in her own terms. "She wears her robes in an odd way," said Tini, "not like we do. If there is anything different in our style, the senior nuns correct it. She is alone with no one to correct her." Not only was she alone, but, I learned many years later (also from Tini who was kind-hearted, tireless, and loved to talk), she was also the most senior nun in Nepal, first among all the living women of the Theravada tradition there. In the Buddhist orders, all monks are considered senior to nuns, but in Pokhara there were no monks. Just Dharmamitra. As we sat having tea by the window overlooking her gate, she told me she had grown up in the big compound across the street. Her family was not Buddhist but Hindu. Pokhara had then been a town of Newars, one of the many prosperous trading centers that caste had established.

*   *   *

When she was a girl, some missionary monks traveling across India to the Himalayas had come to Pokhara. There is an open area near a temple in Pokhara where the long street of the bazaar curves around to run toward the lake. In the embrace of that nook, holy men preach and townspeople gather to hear them. The open space is bare, but there is a large, old peepul tree that spreads its branches over it like a gnarled canopy. The leaves of the tree rustle and sound like rain when the wind blows. As an adolescent listening with her family in the evening after supper, Dharmamitra was moved by the monks' message and by their quiet presence. "I want to become like them," she told her parents, and they laughed. They were a wealthy Hindu family, important in the town. To hear the teachings of holy men was good. To send your daughter to be a nun in a foreign religion was bizarre. In orthodox Hinduism it is a sin to have an unmarried daughter. Each time her cycle passes without seed to make possible a birth, her father is culpable. All those lives crying out to be born, lives to add to the lineage, lives to fulfill the obligation of descendants to the ancestors, lost for lack of a husband. The virgin girl must be given as a gift to the groom's family. This is her father's duty. It is there that she will fulfill her destiny as a woman, that she will come to fruition. Until then the family guards and nurtures her, and as she grows they plan for her marriage.

Behind the walls of the family compound, Dharmamitra grew tall and slim. She had a long face, long eyes and high cheekbones, like a Modigliani painting. Even as an old woman, she was elegant, spare and uncontrived like her bare, shaved head, its lines all revealed. When she was thirteen, her mother told her it was time to marry. She refused. Her father insisted. She was large for her age and angular. She bound her breasts, dressed in boy's clothing, and ran away to find the monks. They took her in and taught her and many months later she returned home a nun. For her parents it was as though she had returned from the dead. They accepted her vocation: perhaps the gods had ordained this. Later they endowed her with the house and garden, a vihar instead of a dowry.

*   *   *

As the sole Theravada monastic in Pokhara, Dharmamitra had independence and she had authority. There were no monks over her, no senior nuns. People called her *Guruma*, "revered teacher." In contrast to the one in Kathmandu, the community that came to her temple was mixed. There was a widow who came with her daughters from a nearby Gurung village to make offerings and ask advice about family affairs. There was some tension with her late husband's brothers, questions about the daughters' marriages. An old man who had been a minister in the democratic government under King Tribhuvan visited often. He and Dharmamitra had fought the Ranas together, and they talked and laughed at length. He was also Gurung and joked about villagers' mixed-up use of formal speech: "My lord the dog has graciously entered the house and the king has also come in." There would be long, interesting afternoons of tea and conversation when he visited, other visitors included as they came in, sometimes a card game with the nephew.

A group of Japanese Nichiren Buddhists had discovered the vihar and befriended Dharmamitra. Sometimes a nun or two from their group would come to stay, going out early each morning for rounds of robust chanting as they marched through the town. They knew only a little Nepali and communicated mainly with smiles and bows. Usually I was in and out around the edges of Dharmamitra's life. I felt welcome and safe on the mats in front of the Buddha, petting her little dog and joining in the conversations that wove their way through the afternoon. Once in a while she invited me to spend the night and I would sleep in a cozy bedroll on the carpet below her bed. I discovered then that the Newar worshipers came late, after supper. The room filled with them, while I lay like a caterpillar in a cocoon. A tall, handsome man set up a harmonium and for hours he played and the crowd sang devotional songs like those I had heard wafting from temples in Kathmandu. Those had been for Hindu gods. These were for the Buddha. I drifted off to sleep hearing the wheezing tones of the instrument and the cadence of the voices while the lights around the Buddha statue cast a rainbow glow across his plaster robes.

Dharmamitra had power. It grew out of chance, daring, and her imagination. Sneaking out of the house as a boy was like jumping off the edge of the earth. She found the monks. They accepted her. Her parents accepted her vocation. They had means. Their generosity provided her place and a position of respectability. She had a following but she dealt with them with a light touch. She was welcoming, not pretentious. She had a ready laugh. Her robes were different in that they slightly resembled a sari in the way they were wrapped: distinctive, but close to normal women's dress. She was decent, thoughtful, and kind, keenly intelligent and effective. All these qualities attracted people to the vihar. They secured donors for the girls' school, a line of buildings above the river that provided possibilities for girls who would have been secluded in the family compound as she had been. The Japanese were taken with her. The Nichiren Buddhists donated money to build a cement meditation hall in a grassy area next to the vihar, an extension of her complex. They wanted to build a peace stupa, a domed temple, near the lake and were planning that in conjunction with Dharmamitra and the old minister. Governmental permission was denied, however, and the old minister was placed in a Kathmandu jail— dark and dirty, no decent food unless brought by the prisoner's family— for conspiring to build an unauthorized temple. Dharmamitra and the minister's wife were distraught. He had diabetes and a heart condition. His name went on the Amnesty International list, but he languished for eighteen months before the government released him. Dharmamitra's power was limited and local.

I found the meditation hall completely unattractive. Its great square cement mass detracted from the lush intricacy of the street. It contrasted with the graceful tile-roofed Newar homes. It went beyond ethnic distinctiveness. Carved windows, sloping roofs, upper-story porches outside the kitchen, these were markers of a Newar house. The meditation hall was modern. This was clear from the cement facing. It was important. This was clear from its size. It was international. No decorative touches marked an association with a particular style. Thankfully, it was only used for formal gatherings and visiting monks. Dharmamitra's life went on as usual in her small house with the plaster Buddha and her dog.

With the meditation hall and all that it signified, though, Dharmamitra's power assumed a different relationship with the world. She was quite consistently herself. Her warmth and style of hospitality did not alter, nor did its breadth. Makers of offerings and singers of hymns still came and concern and gentle advice were still dispensed locally. But her ties to the wealthy Japanese were strong. Her reputation grew and more traveling monks and nuns from abroad came through Pokhara. The monastic institutions in Kathmandu took an interest in her, sometimes friendly, sometimes critical. Someone knew how to let the Amnesty people know about the minister. I thought of the queen coming to cut the ribbon for the school so long ago. Dharmamitra had always had good political sense. Now she had a wider field in which to use it.

I was a stray rather than a node in her network of connections. She never asked me for anything. When I made offerings, she said, "Too much." In the Buddhist tradition, the laity offer gifts to the monastics, whose teaching and way of life are gift enough to the world. When I gave her presents, she gave me others in return. I have a tall brown dresser in my room with a Buddhist altar on top. The dresser is stuffed with pretty clothes. Among them are two blouses sewn in the Newari style, one gold and red with a netted overlay—traditional cloth—and the other smooth pink Japanese polyester, each given by Dharmamitra. "This might look nice on you," she would say as she took it out of her wooden chest, or "The cloth was not quite right for me."

She always welcomed me warmly, but when I thought of living nearby for a while and studying the vihar, she discouraged me. "I don't think that would be so good for you." When I thought of writing her biography, she said, "I wrote that up in Hindi once. I'll give you a copy." When I said I would like to learn more about her life and views and write them down, she said, "Next time you come back to Nepal we'll do that. I should have more time then." As she did not want me to be anthropologist to her, she did not want to be revered teacher to me. The unorthodox flow of gifts testified to that, and the day I bowed to her in the garden as we parted for the afternoon and called her Guruma, as I had heard others do, she hugged me and said, "Not that. You should call me 'friend.'" So I sat at the edge of her card games, and I watched the cement structure go up, and I saw the ebb and flow of people in her world, and I too flowed and ebbed, down the mountain then back to the village. When I came to Pokhara, after I set down my bag the first place I went to was Dharmamitra's.

I returned in the summer of 1987 after an absence of five years. I was pregnant, my daughter a tiny fish in my womb. I thought this time perhaps I could work on her life, taking her "maybe next time" of my previous visit more literally than it was likely meant. I liked the idea of turning her life over in my mind, savoring her experiences, thinking about what they all meant in a larger picture. Buddhist practice was a matter close to my heart. I felt so peaceful in the little temple and was greedy for long afternoons with her, our conversations punctuated by the lowing of the little cow out back. I imagined her eyes round with pleasure when I entered the gate and the happiness of our greetings. "Oh-ho," she had said the first time I returned from the United States. "Oh-ho," holding my shoulders. "You've come. You've come." I cried with joy.

A day or two after arriving in Kathmandu, I saw some orange-robed nuns in the old bazaar. Eager for news of Dharmamitra, I greeted them. They were elderly Newar women and spoke very little Nepali.

"Do you know Dharmamitra?" I asked. They stared at me. They both shrank back against the pillars of a nearby shop. I must have seemed like a strange, inquisitive tourist.

"Don't understand," the more forward one answered.

"Dharmamitra from Pokhara," I said.

"Pokhara? The nun there?" the forward one asked.

"Yes," I said.

"Died," said the old woman.

I stared at her. My voice dropped to a whisper. "Died," I said. "Died?" I was incredulous. The wooden storefronts along the street looked like a scene from a nightmare. "Died?" I repeated. "When did she die?" The nuns leaned together and looked at me, silent. The shopkeeper stepped up, moving in from the background, his eyes soft with compassion. He said something to them in Newari.

"She died about six months ago," he said. "Go with them and they will take you to people who know more."

They proceeded through the bazaar and I followed like a chastened dog. The quiet nun was going to get her nieces for a lesson of some kind at one of the vihars. We walked down narrow backstreets faced with tall brick walls, their regularity broken in places by double doors. We entered through a set of these and found ourselves in a large airy courtyard paved with stones. On three sides were the walls of a house that was built around the courtyard, five stories high. The long eaves of the tiled roof dipped up gracefully at the corners. The dark brown window frames and lintels of the door were ornately carved, sinuous against the red brick. It was shady and quiet. The nun went in and came out with two girls in long braids. I followed them down a maze of streets. Finally we came to a more open area with some newer buildings and entered one of these. There were rooms with blackboards and long tables. A few nuns were grouped around another who seemed to be advising them. One of the girls chatted with me in careful English while we waited. When the nuns finished their session and took the girls out, the ones I had come with led me up to the woman who had been advising the others. They spoke in rapid

Newari. I heard Dharmamitra's name and felt my stomach contract as I looked around the bland schoolroom. I wanted to stay calm. The place seemed so dull and orderly, colorless. From the window I could see the straight lines of the wide streets, the square cement houses. It was a new neighborhood, planned and functional.

The nuns who had brought me bowed and went out. I was alone with this authoritative woman with a shaved head and glasses. She looked at me, her eyes framed by the black plastic rims.

"They tell me you are a friend of Dharmamitra," she said.

"Yes," I replied. "I was so sorry to hear of her death. I just arrived from America a few days ago. I had no idea she had been ill."

"She had cancer," the woman said. "She had been ill for some time before she died. Now we are trying to make arrangements for the vihar. We quickly ordained a woman from Pokhara and want her to take it over. Under our supervision, of course. She is not very well educated. There is also a newly ordained monk, a local man. Some people there think he should run it, but we put the nun in place right away."

I felt fatigue and a sense of vertigo, waves of grief and nausea. Her voice faded in and out. I stood there politely, listening to her well-focused words and watching her strategies unfold. I remembered Dharmamitra's laugh and her little dog. There was a bustle by the door and three nuns stepped in, the one in the front a little rounder and shorter than the others. "Why, you've come!" she said, walking up and taking my hand. My eyes filled with tears. It was Tini.

"Don't worry, I'll be your Guruma now," she said as she led me down the street toward her house. "You know, everything was done for Dharmamitra. When the Japanese Buddhists learned that she was sick, they flew her to Japan for an operation." She opened the door to her small, square house and let me in. It was made of cement, painted blue and white inside. The windows had neat, round bars running across the bottom halves. She beckoned me to a cushioned mat on the floor and came back with a photo album.

"See, I have pictures," she said. "Unfortunately they did not know she was ill until it had been going on for some time. Look, here she is on the bus. They had a whole bus fixed up with a bed and a nurse to take her to

Kathmandu to the plane. Everyone came to see her off. You can just see her face through the window there. They raised her pillow so she could see. Those are oxygen tubes." Her voice lowered. "She smoked, you know. And her robes were always a bit odd." She continued. "Well, she stayed in Japan two or three months and they did everything for her but they could not make her well. The disease had set in too far. So finally they brought her home again. People met the bus with flowers and they brought her to lie in her own bed in the vihar. She only lived a couple of weeks after that. People lined up in the street to file past her bed and say good-bye. She was too weak to talk by then. She just looked at them and tears poured down her cheeks. Of course, she wasn't sad for herself, only for the sorrow her death would cause others. A nun, after all. She just kept crying as they all streamed past, her face still and the tears running from her eyes, flowing and flowing. Very compassionate. I'll make you some tea."

As Tini bustled in the kitchen, I imagined Dharmamitra at home. I could picture the light coming into her room. There was a window overlooking the back garden next to her bed. I used to sleep near it in my bedroll. I remembered little bits of conversation in the dark.

"Shall we sleep now?" she would say, after a while.

"OK."

Then silence, the stars outside. The cow might rustle in her shelter or Silk pad across the room, then I would hear the soft, deep rhythm of Dharmamitra's breathing and drift off to sleep. I looked at the final picture of her taken on the bus. Her face was blurry behind the glass, and the tubes led down into the darkness.

Finally I left Tini's warm hospitality and returned to my hotel. The halls reeked of a cleaning fluid whose odor seemed to be perceptible only to women in the early stages of pregnancy. A kindly assistant manager had paced the halls with me a few days before, trying his best to detect some hint of this smell I insisted was overpowering. I opened the door and turned on the light. Two beds with green spreads, a table, a large window, gauzy curtains drawn. I opened them and looked out on the city unveiled. I went in the bathroom and threw up. Then I lay down on the bed and sobbed, seeing Silk and the cow and banana trees and the kind laughing eyes of my friend; now those eyes streaming with tears, compassion for others' sorrow, yes, and a well-spring of grief for her own death. How could someone who lived so well not mourn life's loss? Waves of sadness washed through my body as I buried my face in the pillow and cried. I felt a run of movements, like bubbles in my stomach. Blind in the dark, deep under the waves, my baby swam.

→ Realizes she isn't going to be
Gurung - She's American

7.
Shattered Worlds and Shards of Love

Memories swirl around, pulling at me like an undertow. There is no direction when I move in these. I made four trips to Nepal. Currents of early and later ones flow together, then separate. Sometimes I look out on the rhythms and undulations and have a sense of control, paddling in the midst of them. Other times they wash over me and I am lost, no still point, no center, just waves of images, longing, pain.

How could I have left? I went with my friend Saras one day to her plot of soybeans and sweet peas. The peas were ripening and we picked them, sitting and crunching a few at intervals. Her sisters had married men in the high-paying British army and led exciting lives: sojourns in Hong Kong, plans for houses in the town. Her husband was in India and they saved and were careful. Their household was separate from the extended family and so Saras farmed their plots alone. Near her home village there was a woman, old now, she said, but once very lovely. She had come from a wealthier country, perhaps Burma, and had been a nurse there or a teacher. She had married a Gurkha soldier and come to live in the mountains, a hard life for her. She worked the land and cared for the house just as they did, never returning home. A quiet woman, well-liked, part of their world now. She could embroider designs, Saras said, beautiful vivid colors flowing across the cloth. "Never returned home," I thought. "That could be me."

People teased me about marrying a cross-cousin, the category of relative one flirts with and who has first claim on a girl as wife. I would turn aside smiling and pull my shawl close. "Don't marry anyone here, Ernestine," Ama would say. "You can't work hard enough. He'd gobble up your money and then throw you out." I felt married to the land, as though it were my body and my blood. I bathed in the cold streams and walked the rocky paths and squished up to my knees in the rice paddies pushing the small plants into the mud. My body fell into rhythm with the days and the seasons.

Everything shatters. What can you hold on to? It moves and changes, a flow of lives. It all started with the large green boxes. I was sitting at Amrit Kumari's store in Dusam, drinking tea with my friends and watching people go by on the trail. The hot weather of March had broken, the stifling air cleared by occasional thunderstorms. Fat puffy clouds floated above the mountains and sailed through the gorge. The day was pleasant and breezy. We had come to get odds and ends: matches, batteries, some cloth for a blouse. Some men from the village were playing cards in the corner with Tika Prasad. His mules roamed out back on the fields. As we sipped our tea, we heard a steady stamping sound. Curious, we peered down the trail. A column of men rounded the bend, dressed in dark green fatigues.

Amrit Kumari straightened her back and squinted at them. "Where are you going?" she called out.

A man in the front stopped and leaned against the stone resting place in front of her shop. Men carrying long green boxes, like trunks, rounded the bend behind him. "We are headed up toward Jomsom," he said.

"What for?" she asked.

"Training," he replied. They carried the insignia of the Nepalese army.

"What's in the boxes?" she asked.

"Medical supplies," he replied. I looked at the boxes now that a file of men had stopped behind him. In black printed letters one read, "grenades." Another read "ammunition." He looked at me. "What's that?" he asked.

"A white woman," said Amrit Kumari.

"What's she doing here?" he asked.

"Learning the language, studying the customs," replied Amrit Kumari. I pulled my shawl around and gazed out over the fields.

He signaled to the line of men behind him. "Let's go," he said, and they moved into order and marched on. I watched the boxes go by. One did say "medical supplies." Others said "artillery."

The line of men and boxes continued for some time. When they passed out of earshot, a man in the card game spoke up. "It's the Tibetans they're after," he said. "The Khampa soldiers." These were men from the province of Kham in Tibet, known for their loyalty to the Dalai Lama and their fierceness in fighting. They waged guerrilla warfare on the Chinese, a thorn in their side, ambushing a convoy here, blowing up an ammunition depot there. "They have a big encampment up by Tilicho Lake, on our side of the border. The Chinese want them out. If the Nepalese government doesn't clear the camps, the Chinese will come in and do it themselves. That's what I hear," he said.

For days soldiers marched, more and more of them in green fatigues going up the trail. People in the village were edgy, wondering what it would come to in the end. Since Jomsom itself was five days' walk from Tebas and Tilicho Lake several days above that, there did not seem to be any immediate danger to us. I worried about Maila lama and his family, living so near Jomsom itself. Ama's friends, Amre and Ammaili, joked nervously about the troops. "I don't want to see a war," Amre said. "It's all right for you. The young women they'll carry off to sleep with, but we old ones, they'll just kill us on the spot." People worried about their friends and relatives further north. Travel was limited. An officer was posted in Big Rock, a village about an hour up the trail. The area from Cliff Shelter north was closed to tourists. Police at the checkpoint there turned back any strays.

The area had been closed to foreigners for over a month before I knew about it. Bhimsen told me. It was Saturday and guards at the checkpoint were relaxed. They seemed not to notice me go by at all. I told Ama when I got home that they were not allowing tourists in the area. "I know," she said. "Apa has told the officer in Big Rock that you belong to us and he's letting you stay for now. Just stay around quietly. And if I were you, I'd go to Big Rock and cultivate the man. Pay your respects and buy him a cup of tea or two." I felt uneasy. The officer was haughty and sarcastic, at least to me. I could not imagine going to pay him a social call. I felt the tenuousness of my position and resented it.

The monsoon was coming. We had had weeks of thunderstorms. The thunder echoed in the gorge and the cool rain pounded down, then the winds carried the storm away, the thunder becoming fainter, rain softer. The walls of the gorge were high, maybe two thousand feet above the river. The storm would hit the other side, then the reverberations would grow louder as the storm returned, bouncing off the steep walls of the mountains. This would happen again and again as the storms spent themselves, thunder and rain amplified, then fading, then amplified again as the storms oscillated through the gorge.

The monsoon was different. It came from the south, a wall of warm water. It was steady, sweeping, stately. The water poured down and all one could see was a torrent of wetness. Sometimes even nearby objects were obscured, everything beyond the eaves of the house blurred by sheets of water. It was wet, fecund, fierce, beautiful. I wanted it to go on forever.

The terraces filled with pools of water, mountainsides of mirrors reflecting the sky and the clouds. The little rice seedlings that had been set to sprout in drier earth were transplanted into the wet, silted terraces. We worked in lines, mud oozing through our toes, water to our knees, and poked the little plants into the earth. The terraces turned a new, soft green that looked like the essence of life. The swollen river coursed through the mountains and the rice plants grew.

We heard little of the armies in the north. People who carried news said there had been no fighting but that the Nepali army had cut off the Khampas' supplies, planning to starve them out. I knew an American woman with the Peace Corps who had lived in Dorje. She had a calm, direct manner and listened with a kind of penetrating gentleness and quiet warmth. Slim and graceful with long, blonde hair, she lived there and taught the schoolchildren. The leader of the Khampas, Wangde, came down to that area regularly and liked to sit and talk with her. One night he brought a horse and asked her to come away with him. I imagine it dark, the wind catching her hair, veiling her for a moment. She refused. By the time the armies marched up, she was living with friends in a moldering mansion in Kathmandu. Aristocrats fallen on hard times rented out their palaces, gardens gone to seed, creepers crawling across the windows, shutters hanging askew, but still elegant. This is where I met her, a friend of friends. This is where she was living, I think, when she heard that Wangde, fleeing east across the Himals with a company of men, had been shot. Some said it was a rumor to save face for the army since he had evaded capture. Others said it was true. At any rate, the encampment was seized and the Khampas' weapons were captured and placed on display at the parade ground in Kathmandu. American-made, people said, supplied by the CIA.

After dinner one evening, Ama sent me down to Prema lama's house to return a pot to his adopted mother. I sat by the hearth with them for a few minutes and chatted about the crops and the weather. When I stepped out to go home, Prema followed me.

"I am going to Pokhara in a couple of days, if you need company," he said. "I have some business there." I was puzzled. He looked at me. "You know the officer said you have to leave?"

I felt numb and backed off into the twilight. "Go? No," I said. "I did not know."

"In a day or two," he said. "I'll walk down with you."

I walked past the buffalo, drooling as it ate its feed. The stable had a pungent animal smell, damp straw and droppings. I climbed up the footholds in the wall and stood in the empty courtyard. The sky was the luminous deep blue of late evening, bright against the mountains. A star or two was out. The mountains were dark masses, a palpable presence, still but teeming with life. A light flickered across the gorge. "Witch's fire," I remembered Ama saying. I thought it might just as well be a glimmer of a hearth fire through a window, people cooking their dinner, looking forward to a meal after a long day's work. I felt the darkness wrap around me like a shawl. The corn was drying on a raised rack nearby. I heard the goats shuffle in their shelter. Some kids and a baby buffalo were tied up on the porch. I turned toward the glow of the open door and went in.

"What is it?" Ama said.

My voice was low. "The lama told me," I said, "I have to go."

"That ass pushes in everywhere," Apa said. "Tomorrow is the festival for the new month. A special one this time, a little celebration, offerings for the ancestors. We wanted you to enjoy it without sadness in your heart. Now look what he's done."

I looked at the flickering flames of the fire, the coals underneath glowing deep red. Tson was stirring a batter for pastries and a deep pan of hot oil sat on the tripod. She took a handful of batter and swirled a circle of it through her fingers into the oil. It popped and sizzled. She dipped it out and swirled another one in. It was special food for the offerings.

"Try some," said Ama, handing me a warm circle. It was crisp on the outside, chewy within, and tasty. I sat with them a while and then got up to go to bed. Ama rose and walked me to my room.

"Sleep now," she said lightly touching my arm.

"I'll sleep," I said obediently, hesitating under her touch, wanting to stay near her. I thought with regret of all the times I had been troublesome. I looked at her face outlined in the moonlight. Then I turned and walked through the door to my bed. The wooden shutter that blocked my window was closed and the darkness was inky. I lay against the cotton mattress and the wood breathing in the smells of the place, listening to the sounds and eventually, as I had promised, I fell asleep.

In the morning, I prepared my belongings for the trip to Pokhara, enough for a long stay, but not everything. The ceremony was brief and exuberant, just our household, Apa hailing the new month. I felt like I was watching it from a vast distance. After breakfast, the officer showed up.

"When might I be able to return?" I asked him.

He looked at me. "It's hard to say," he said. "The area could remain permanently closed." I imagined the mountains closing up behind me as I left. This was before my sisters moved to the town, before the fabric of village life began to fray. The world that I knew there in the village existed only over the mountains and across the rivers that were going to be forbidden to me now. Its boundaries made it whole, and I was placed outside them. Foreigners were to be prohibited from entering even Cliff Shelter. I looked at the ground, feeling hollow inside. I looked out at the mountains, around at the stone houses. I felt trapped. Prema lama strode into the courtyard, a bag slung over his shoulder. "Let's go," he said. I bowed to Ama and Apa and followed him out the gate. The two of us, who did not belong, walked down the mountain on the great twisting line of stone steps to the river. He could return at will, but I could not.

*   *   *

I was not the only one displaced, evicted from what I had wrongly taken for granted. Ama's mother died, and that was a loss that went further and deeper than anyone would have imagined. A few months before the green boxes went north into the mountains, I came home and Apa said to me, "Your mother cannot eat salt." She was sitting in the shadows. I was puzzled. Apa must have seen that I did not get the point. "Her mother has died," he said. "We got the news today from Kathmandu." Close relatives abstain from salt for a period of time after a death as a sign of mourning.

Later I heard her talking to others, crying and saying, "He didn't even call me for the cremation." Her brother had taken their mother to the hospital in Kathmandu for treatment, and had not sent word to her until after the body had been cremated. She had not been there to send her mother into the fire. She wept. I did not know this uncle Neem Bahadur well. He was small with a narrow face, slim and agile but deliberate in his movements. He had an air of skepticism about him and was not given to elaborate, gracious greetings or warm conversation. He kept to himself. His wife was talkative at times but tended to snub people of lower status. She did not quite know what to make of me and was friendly at some moments and haughty at others. He treated me like an oddity.

While a cremation can take place near any river, a funeral, the *pae*, should be held at one's home. The daughter and son are both essential to the ritual. Since they were a high ranking family, it was to be a great ceremony with several lamas and hundreds of guests. It was held at the house in Torr that we had visited when we last saw Ama's mother, their lineage home. Ama, Tson, and assorted friends and neighbors spent days cooking before we left, making various pastries and other delicacies to present as offerings. Ama also commissioned Tej lama to make the effigy. While most lamas made a bamboo frame structure wrapped with cloth, Tej made effigies of clay, life-size and life-like. The effigy houses the spirit for the duration of the ceremony, until the canopy covering the ritual area is pulled back and the spirit sent off by the lamas. When Tej made an effigy, it looked as though the dead person had returned, presiding behind the large platform on which food and flowers were placed, garlanded with rupee notes to give as gifts when the spirit reached the land of the ancestors and they asked, "What have you brought us?" One always gives presents on arriving from a journey.

Our trip to Torr was quick this time, and we entered not the meandering back way, but up the main path into the village. Ama was wearing her best sari and was decked with gold. What happened next surprised me. From courtyards along the way, people came to the path and bowed down before her, placing their heads on her feet. "No need," she would say touching their heads, or, "May you have long life; may you be well." It was like wind bending the barley stalks, all these people bowing before her, one by one, as we proceeded up the path. They were honoring the dignity of her aristocratic family, and of her person. I was stunned as I walked along behind. She was poised but seemed moved, balanced but intent as she walked toward the house that was without a mother now. Her brother greeted her briefly when she arrived.

Later that night, the ceremony began with resounding drumbeats and the lamas dancing, their shadows cast huge by the light of the lantern. The effigy was installed and by midmorning the next day the usual ritual activities were underway: shamans singing the ancient songs to guide the soul, lamas chanting the sacred texts, guests arriving in hordes and being given tea and snacks, liquor for the men. I watched and listened, sitting in the different venues, chatting with relatives and friends. It was a familiar process now, the unfolding funeral. Ama was busy tending to the offerings and Apa when not helping was off among the important men. I drifted and observed. The shamans made a little space near them for me to sit. They were brothers and I had watched them work several times before. The slow rhythm of their recitations was hypnotic, comforting, punctuated now and then by a strike on the drum. As afternoon wore on, their lulling music was interrupted by the sound of harsh words across the courtyard. I looked over but stayed out of the way. Ama stood aside looking distressed. Apa was speaking vehemently. I could not catch the words. After the turmoil died down I edged over. A few men from our village stood in a knot. The others had gone inside. It was clearly not my place to follow.

"What happened?" I asked one of the men.

"Neem Bahadur replaced the effigy," he said.

"The effigy Ama brought?" I asked.

"Yes," he said. "He had the lamas from Torr make another and replace it. He threw it aside. After the ritual had already begun. It is like throwing away the spirit's body," he said, becoming agitated.

"Why did he do that?" I asked.

"Perhaps it was sick," he said impatiently and turned aside.

I felt confused and puzzled. It was clearly a grievous insult to the family, a public humilation of Ama, a wound to the spirit of the deceased, installed in a body only to lose it. The rest of the funeral was steeped in a hum of discussion about the incident. Worse things were to come.

Ama was shaken after the funeral but seemed to recover little by little after we returned home. Tson's baby was plump and charming and gave her much pleasure. It was the dry time of winter. Work was light. The rivers were low and people visited across the bamboo footbridges and fords. Vultures and great birds of prey wheeled in the gorges below the village, the sun burnishing their wings. Ama and Apa had put me in a little ancillary house at the end of their courtyard and I enjoyed the privacy and space, though with much of life lived outdoors all I did inside was sleep and type my notes.

One day I returned from checking my mail at Cliff Shelter and crossed the courtyard to find my door wide open. Ama was lying on my bed with her head in her arms and Atay, Apa's brother's wife, was making tea.

"Why is Ama here?" I asked.

"Hush. Sit down," said Atay. She poured me a glass of tea and brought one to Ama.

Ama turned away. "My brother has killed me," she said. I noticed there were bundles of things from the house on the floor, bedrolls in the corner. Ama cried and talked softly. She refused the tea.

Atay sat next to her on the cot. "Don't cry. Don't cry," she said. "No one knows what is written in their destiny. Now you have to suffer. Don't cry."

Little by little the story came out. Apa had gone to a meeting in another village. Neem Bahadur had come with his wife and children and been received at the house by Ama. He had told her she could no longer live in that house, that it was his inheritance. Their father had been rich. Neem Bahadur already had houses in Torr and in Pokhara, another in a more distant town. Their father had given land in Tebas and the grand house there to Ama. The land he had deeded to her. Neem Bahadur was nearly grown when he gave her the house. "Do not deed it," he said. "I prefer it to be a gift from my own hand, since it comes from my patrimony." The father acquiesced. When the father died, Neem Bahadur demanded the house. Ama was derisive and said it was hers, a gift from their father. Their mother was shocked and rebuked him. Now their mother was dead and there was no one to restrain him. When Ama again refused to leave, he began throwing her things onto the courtyard. The children were there and Tson with the baby. Ama was afraid for them and left the house. Neem Bahadur spent the night there with his family and returned the next day to Torr, leaving a large padlock on the door. "Even the fine dishes, we had to leave behind," Ama said. "Now we'll live in this little place. That's all right," she said, her voice trailing off.

I had noticed brothers quarreling with sisters after funerals before, accusing them of being given goods that were rightfully part of their patrimony. Two little boys taunted me on windswept path once: "Can we touch your breasts? When you die, they'll throw you away and you'll give all your wealth to a daughter." Traditionally men inherit the family wealth. But parents are ambivalent. The son is expected to care for his aging parents, though parents do not trust this and fear neglect. "Daughters are more loving," I heard many parents say. "They are always affectionate but sons lose their love for their parents after they marry." A growing distance between sons and parents is expected. Sons are coddled while daughters work harder and from an earlier age. But the balance changes later, perhaps fostering resentment. Married daughters return and are pampered. It is their time to rest and find relief from the endless tasks assigned by their mothers-in-law. There is a special pleasure in the company of a loved, returned child. Neighbors come to visit and admire the daughter's clothes and jewelry which show the status of her husband's family and the esteem in which she is held there. I could imagine Neem Bahadur growing up in the shadow of his sister. He was unprepossessing in looks and manner. She was lovely, witty, poised. She had been the heir apparent for twelve years, until he arrived and she was married. As an only child, she had not been so strongly expected to have the kind of humility demanded of women. She was conscious of her honor, forthright and intelligent. She grew up to be a charismatic woman. I remembered the people bowing along the path, their sincerity and her grace.

He had not been much nurtured by her, since she had married in his infancy. Perhaps nurturance would have softened his rage, perhaps not. I imagine that she seemed to him an intruder in his childhood home, coming and absorbing attention and affection he felt to be rightfully his. Unlike the house itself, he could not wrench these back. She may have resented him, occupying the home from which she had been ejected. Then in middle-age when she least expected it, she was ejected from her home again.

The Gurung world for all its true graciousness is suffused with fear and resentment. Hopes for nurturance are high. Promises of it abound, but people are drained by the demands of social obligation, disappointed by social illusions. Promises must be made that cannot always be kept. Absolute belonging is promised but cannot be realized. Complete nurturance is promised but cannot be relied upon. Pleasing deceptions paper over the cracks and the world has a lovely aesthetic, but it seethes. This is the passion, tension, dynamism of their universe. It is alive but it is not safe.

She could skate through the danger. Socially agile, she could play. Hungry for honor, she could calculate. He sat on his wealth, bloated and brooding. Then he struck her. Ama never recovered. Her heart-mind had shrunk, people said. She could not quite rise up to meet life, though she went through the motions. Grand gestures of honor were not possible from her little house. She seemed fundamentally herself, but contracted, bruised. She smoked more and drank too much. I went to sleep in the storeroom at the end of the veranda. It had a little window overlooking the path and the buffalo shed. This is where I was when the monsoon swept up the valley and the officer came to see that I left Tebas.

*   *   *

In Pokhara, the rains poured down, pounding on the roof above the upper-story room in which I slept. Prema lama stayed a few days, then returned. I lay in the dark those nights, listening to his breathing across the room and watching the street through the window. Sleep escaped me. Dharmamitra gave me company and comfort, and someone along the way, maybe Bhimsen's brother who lived in the bazaar, suggested I go to see the provincial governor.

I was daunted. He was a man from the capital. I was young with only my village clothes, nothing sophisticated or respectable. I looked out at the mountains veiled with clouds, dusky where they showed through against the gray sky. They seemed soft with the summer wetness, rounded and verdant. I took a taxi to the administrative complex down by the airport. They were a series of bungalows, whitewashed with red windows, the flag flying outside and over the door the same insignia I had seen on the green boxes. I asked a soldier on guard which was the office of the governor. He pointed me toward a large central structure.

The office was quiet. Administrative life seemed to slow down in the rainy season, as farm work speeded up. Clerks directed me to the governor's personal assistant. He was a young, serious-looking man, thin and sincere. He asked my business and as I began the story, the governor himself emerged from his office. He was portly with glasses, and had a genial face but moved with the gravity of an Important Person. He asked his assistant what my business was about.

"Some matter from a village," the young man replied.

"Come in," said the governor.

I was shocked. I followed him into a large office with bookcases and a big square carpet. He sat behind his desk and motioned me to take a chair. I thought, "This is the governor's office. I am speaking with the governor." I looked at my hands. He asked me kindly about where I had been living and I told him about the village and then with his encouragement told him how I had been sent out, not knowing when I could return, and how I wished to go back. My voice was strained.

"I don't see that he needed to send you out," he said. I looked up. "Give it a week or two," he continued, "and then go back. I'll write you a letter." I was filled with gratitude. I was speechless. I stared at his carpet.

"I am deeply grateful," I said.

He told me my Nepali was good but that it was odd that my accent was more rural than foreign. "You sound like a hill-woman," he said smiling. "My wife and daughter would like to meet you. Come to dinner." Dharmamitra had already invited me, so I declined apologetically, saying I had already accepted an invitation from a friend. His face tensed and he dropped the subject. I felt I had missed something about the etiquette of Important Persons. As we left the office, he instructed the assistant to write the letter and I waited outside with the clerks until it was ready, then carried it off, complete with red seal. Dharmamitra and I had a truly fine meal.

Having thought I might be leaving the village forever, I was in Pokhara little more than a month. In summer, Pokhara is fully tropical, lush and sultry. Water runs down the street. Walls and shoes become furry with mold. Bugs proliferate. Plants flourish. Clumps of flowers bulge from their beds and push through fences. Creepers wind around great trunks of trees and travel across their branches. I was exhausted from the tension of having been forced to leave the village. It shattered a fiction I had counted on, the fiction of belonging. No matrix of kinship, no affectionate ties, no understanding of honor had been able to protect me. Their world was part of me, like my rural accent and my dreams (in Nepali without subtitles, filled with tigers and jungles), but it owed me nothing. I had no claim.

Weak and depressed, I got sick. It was not a flamboyant illness, just a quiet one, draining my strength. It was a typical summer stomach problem, a low-grade dysentery, but it did not respond to medication. I lost interest in going out much and lay in bed reading or looking out the window at life on the street. Sometimes I went to see Dharmamitra. The rain poured down but it did not have the thrill of great billowy clouds sweeping up the gorge. It sounded different on the tin roofs of the bazaar. Finally the date on the governor's letter arrived and I packed my things to return.

I was glad to be back in the village but felt unsettled. I remained ill and was irritable. It was hard for me to eat. The rice ripened, turning the terraces golden. It was harvested and laid out in the courtyard where oxen tethered to a stake walked slowly round and round, crushing the hard husks and freeing the brown kernels. After they had done their patient work, we sat in a circle and beat it with bamboo sticks. The air filled with blonde dust and little bits of chaff. Then it was winnowed, tossed up so the wind caught the bits of husk and the heavier kernels fell back down and were deftly slid into a waiting basket and another heap lifted and tossed with a wide woven circlet.

After the rice was harvested, the mountains looked bare, brown on brown broken by jungle and villages here and there. The air was crisp and clear. The Dasain festival approached. Ama and Apa cultivated new green barley sprouts in a dark corner of the house. These were for the ritual. A mountain goat was tethered in the courtyard. When I washed my face in the morning it would carry off the soap dish and I would chase it to retrieve it, then scratch its shaggy head. After a number of days it felt like a family pet. The idea of sacrifice moved to the back of my mind. A large wooden swing was set up at the back of the village and the young men and women and older children went up each evening and played on it.

The festival day itself began early. *Das* means ten and it is the tenth day of a series of smaller rituals commemorating the victory of good over evil. In much of Nepal it is conceived of as the celebration of the goddess Durga vanquishing a demon so dreadful that none of the gods could subdue it.

Apa told me it commemorated the victory of Ram, a great prince and an incarnation of the god Vishnu, over the evil Ravana, a demon made strong through ascetic practices who, filled with lust, had abducted Ram's lovely wife Sita. Their armies had clashed and Ram, aided by his loyal servant Hanuman, leader of the monkeys, had prevailed after long battle. On this day weapons and tools are blessed through blood sacrifice. The mountain goat was beheaded early and went into the pot as celebratory food. I did not watch.

Dasain restores order to a disordered world. Demons, deities, and princes are put in their places. In the village, the world is also ordered through the ritual. People go for blessing to their elders, bowing down to their feet. The elders place a few barley sprouts behind their ears and a sticky paste of red powder and rice in the middle of their foreheads and give blessings: "May you be well." "May you have high status." "May you marry a colonel or a general." "May you have wealth." "May you live long." "May your heart grow as great as it is able." I went with the other children of the family from house to house of relatives, bowing low and being showered with blessings.

At home people came all day to receive Apa's blessings. Even in the small house, he was still headman. In the past on the night of Dasain called *kalorat*, "black night," untouchables had come to dance in the courtyard of the headman, performing for him and the assembled villagers, and his family had offered a feast to all. This year that was not done, as there was now an elected mayor, who took issue with the idea that the *kalorat* dancing should be done at the headman's house and not at his. Throughout the day there had been suspense about where the dancing would take place and rumors that it would be done at one house, then talk that it would take place at the other. Finally the dancing did not take place at all. The order of life was no longer clear.

The mayor was a relative of Ama's, whose lineage was located in Torr. The family had owned land in Tebas and this was where he settled. Some said he was illegitimate, or the son of a junior wife. His father's lineage was respectable, which is what counts, and he was treated with reasonable regard in Tebas. He was protective of his status and made sure he was always high in lines of seating precedence. He liked to tease me, and was quick to notice my mistakes or to invite me to join a line of precedence that was totally inappropriate, which would have broadcast a shocking lack of modesty had I accepted it. Even before I knew the rules, I sensed that my place was not with high-ranking middle-aged men. At formal gatherings the women's warmth and running commentary were far more interesting. At one large meeting, he had called me forward from a knot of women seated far in the back of the group that filled up the expansive grounds of the local government building. I walked up through a crowd of over a hundred people, confused about what might be expected of me. Others were curious, too, and the hum of conversation hushed. He handed me a colored bank note.

"Tell the people, niece, from which country this money comes," he said. I looked at it. It was pink and yellow and said "50,000 Bucks" in each corner. In the center was printed "Bank of Good Luck." I stood there in the sun with the assembled crowd staring at me, completely bewildered by the turn of events.

"It is not the currency of any country," I said. "It is children's play money." Murmurs ran through the crowd.

"All right, niece," he said, letting me know I was dismissed. I walked back through the crowd and returned to my place with the women.

"Did you know this was coming?" they asked. "Had you seen that note before?"

"No," I replied. "Never. What is all this about?"

They told me that several months before, an untouchable boy, illiterate, had found this note on the trail and had brought it to the mayor to ask how to cash it in. The mayor had kept it and the story had spread that he had stolen a vast amount of foreign currency from this impoverished boy. Corruption was expected of elected officials. In a village near Pokhara, funds for a water system had been given to the mayor three times, and still people had to walk a mile to collect water from a stream that dried to a trickle in the winter. When I asked why the water system had not been installed, they replied philosophically, "Because the mayor ate the money." When I asked how this could be allowed to happen when they so desperately needed fresh water, they replied, "What can one do?" Still, this act seemed extreme, taking a windfall from this child and his family, not even a bribe but the whole thing. People talked. It was not good for his honor.

Now I had shown that the note was worthless. Something dropped by a tourist on the trail, meant to quiet the children who came to the roadside asking for money, pens, or sweets. "The Bank of Good Luck": a bill wafting down to the trail where foreign and local worlds met, creating hope and controversy. The mayor, who had seemed so eager to belittle me, staging this spectacle where I was for a moment conferred with authority: consolidating his position with whatever came to hand, pulling me up as icon of the modern, rational world, come to vindicate him, then sending me back to my place among the women. "But why did he keep the note in the first place?" people asked, still suspicious.

The boundaries of the village had always been porous, penetrable by outsiders. Order had never been fully set. There was movement and change. The headman's lineage had been designated generations earlier as tax collectors by the royal government. That consolidated their position among other clan chiefs. Families rose and fell. People migrated, not just recently to towns or into military service, but hundreds of years ago to new settlements. This was the western edge of Gurung country, settled late, only a few centuries ago. After World War I, cash became important, tea was introduced, the natural resources of the area, such as water, wood, and fodder for the animals, began to dwindle. Life was always shifting. Now there were strange non-currencies appearing, an ambiguous foreigner in the village but not of it, a rationalized electoral system that allowed the ambitious to climb to power, tourists who embodied hitherto unseen possibilities of wealth and leisure. Ideas of comfort and freedom and power, of the security of good health and the open horizons of education, for their children if not for themselves, propelled people away from the center, from the lineage home of the village to choices beyond its borders. Many with wealth left. Many of those who stayed were restless. The coherence of the village unraveled.

This happened gradually. In the early years that I lived there, Apa held a regional elected office that gave him precedence over the mayor, as well as being the traditional headman. His home was the center of village activities, especially when they were still living in the big house. It was the site of village council meetings, the place where travelers were housed, the arena for settling disputes. During the time of my initial stay, from 1973 to 1975, nearly all the wealthy and important families still lived in the village. One man, a World War II hero, had been summoned to Kathmandu by King Tribhuvan to be a minister in his government in the 1950s. He had moved there with his wife and children but made frequent trips back to his lineage home in Tebas and insisted that his children speak Gurung at home in Kathmandu. By the time of my last trip twelve years later, many families had moved to Pokhara and agreed that the children should not speak Gurung lest it disadvantage them in school. The land they left was sharecropped by poorer families, so that the produce of the village did not stay there to sustain its members but a part was carried off to feed those living in the town. In the town itself, though, neighborhoods formed that replicated village ties and there was a style of life that was distinctly Gurung. I stayed a month with my sister in Pokhara and spent most of the time there sitting on her porch with village friends. Who knows what new coherence will emerge, both in the village and beyond it.

Dasain was a celebration of the more familiar kind of coherence, of the benevolence and protection of authority that is conferred and blessed by the gods. These blessings are passed by elders to dependents in the human world in return for their devotion and loyalty. This knits the social fabric together, though people can and do use the ritual idiom to protest. Not coming when expected to bow down ceremoniously and take blessing delivers, very quietly, a powerful statement.

Order costs; coherence does not come free. It is forged from a crucible of impulses and desires. Will and desire are disciplined and refined as a person submits to the obligations of relationship: meeting expectations, curbing self-interest, shaping the passions to fit the avenues created for them, submerging those that do not fit. Life in these terms has grace. As with a dancer whose wildness pulses beneath the restraint of her technique, the grace is there in the tension and skill of having achieved a fit of one's inner self with the social world, a balance of passion and control. Failure results in humiliation or brutality. Success brings honor, which consists of living well within one's status. It brings regard and the right to one's position. One bows down and is blessed: submission to the prevailing order confers belonging and nurture. The order is conceived not just as the human world of authority but as the *dharma*, the law by which the universe, natural and divine, operates. To follow it makes one whole and offers protection. "I cannot be bewitched," Maili said, "because my spirit is harmonious."

The Dasain celebration provides nurture through sacrifice. A water buffalo is brought for the community and people gather to watch it killed. This took place in our courtyard, under the steps to the room where I had first slept. It is considered best if the animal is killed with one strong stroke. A man lifted the large curved knife above his head and tensed his shoulders as he brought it down on the buffalo's neck. Blood spurted. The animal bellowed, eyes rolling. "It's not done," a man called and the sacrificer raised his knife again and, rising up on his toes, brought it down with full force. The head fell to the ground, horns clattering on the stones and a shout went up from the crowd. A pool of blood spread out from the body, dark and wet on the courtyard. Small children shrank back but the older ones ran forward. Seyli dipped her hands in the blood and ran to the door of the house, making handprints along the lintels. This confers protection on the household. Hunks of meat were sliced off the body and placed in brass plates that people held out and then took home for their meals. An untouchable family took the nose. At the end of the day, all that was left was a stain on the stones.

At nightfall, people sit around their hearths. The evening meal is served: heaps of food in wealthier households, the addition of a few extras, like the succulent meat, in the poorer ones. I was tired from all the events of the day, going from house to house to see the relatives, dealing with the long stream of visitors at home. I enjoyed the soft, golden glow of the kerosene lamp. Images of the sacrifice came back to me. I had been disturbed but unable to look away. The meat was strong and sweet in flavor. I was implicated as I chewed. I remembered the body collapsing to the ground, blood flowing everywhere. The blood protected households; the body sustained the people. The order of the world had been affirmed: good over evil. In the Buddhist monasteries of the north, all day long there had been ceremonies to counteract the pain of so much killing. For them the Hindu sacrifice did not further the good. I thought of the animal's frightened eyes. Good was unclear. The moral order was ambiguous. Ama leaned across the fire and offered me more meat, then drank the sauce from her round, brass plate.

I belonged and I did not. I was home and I was not. I could not find the comfort in the village I had felt before being sent out. It became cold and bleak as the year progressed, and I did not recover from my illness. My stomach hurt and I had little appetite for any food. Tired all the time, I had little appetite for life. Though I felt withdrawn, I stubbornly clung to the village. Having reclaimed my place there, I was reluctant to consider leaving. I was still not sure that I wanted to leave at all. Yet I was not fully there. My sense of ease was gone. I was unwell, restless, demanding.

Tebas was the potato capital of the region, the potatoes there being abundant and delicious. They were the main feature of every meal, and during my illness I began to loathe them. Ama promised one day to make some greens with the rice, along with the usual potato curry. I looked forward to the treat all day. Agai was visiting from her husband's home and we gathered around the fire for dinner, brass plates with high sides handed around. Ama served the rice. When she reached out with a ladle of potatoes, I declined, saying I would like to have just the rice and greens. She told me she had not had time to get the greens. I thought of how she had been around the courtyard all day, laughing and playing with little Ratna.

"I am not hungry then," I said, and got up and stormed off to my room.

She followed me and began to cry, "Am I not to play with my little grandson then? Now you are not going to eat?"

I began to cry, too. We sat together for a while and then I went in and had some food. I felt ashamed. The next day Agai went up to the jungle and gathered some mushrooms, saying, "Here, have these. We'll make them into a nice curry for you. They taste delicious." I remembered how remote she had been for the first few months we had known each other. I was moved by the change in her and touched by the trouble she had taken for me.

The demands of day-to-day life do not allow much care to be taken of someone who is ill in the village. As my health continued to decline, I returned to Pokhara to see the doctors at Radiant Hospital, staffed by missionaries. The hospital was efficient and well run, a series of low white buildings near the river. They gave me medicine, but the parasites did not depart. They gave me stronger medicine, with no result. They gave me dangerously strong medicine, and the tests still showed parasites.

"The medicine is not working," said the chief physician, an elderly British woman. I had seen her often in the past, with good results. She was knowledgeable and caring. She sat me down in a wooden chair in her office. "I am sorry, but you must be possessed," she said. "I'm afraid for your life. I'll pray for you, though unless you turn to Christ it will do you little good.

I was dismayed by her diagnosis. Katwale, the shaman, had already determined that I had been possessed by two spirits and a witch. He had tried cures and on checking me after the last one, he had shaken his head and murmured, "Mm. Tenacious." Feeling depressed, I stopped into a tea shop I frequented, near the temple with the spreading peepul tree outside. One of the regulars was a plump, kindly Brahmin man who worked in a government office. I often ran into him there when I was in town. He asked why I seemed so dejected and I told him the story of my consultation with the doctors.

"I can help you," he said. He told me the story of how he had been possessed for some time by powerful spirits who nearly killed him, but he was able to prevail and in overcoming them had learned to manipulate spirits himself.

"He is a powerful shaman," one of the other customers said. "The best." Tom, a Peace Corps volunteer who lived nearby, stopped in and joined us.

"I can talk with the spirits," said the Brahmin. I can discover who they are and what they want. I can make an amulet to keep them away. You need to come to the cremation ground at midnight and bring a chicken. We could meet here and then go down together." It sounded rather alarming to me, going down to the sandy area by the river where the bodies were burned. Dogs roamed there. There were bits of charred wood. I had never been near it. People considered it a dangerous place, especially after dark. I had known the Brahmin for some time and did not fear him, but the whole situation sounded frightening. Still, I was so weak and sick, pronounced possessed by the most respected doctor in town. Here was a virtuoso shaman. Tom said that if I liked he would come, too. The Brahmin's friend said he could procure a chicken to bring. I agreed to meet them back at the tea shop at nine, so we could do the preliminary rituals and then proceed to the river.

The streets were deserted at that time of night, dark except for the light of a weak bulb here or there coming through a window. I walked quickly. The Brahmin and his friend were there with the chicken. Tom showed up a few minutes later. The tea shop owner came and sat with us a few minutes and then went up to put her children to bed. The tea shop was a wooden extension of her house, with two or three wooden tables with benches. The front was usually open, but since it was late and the shop was closed, large wooden doors had been pulled across and shut. The Brahmin said the chicken needed to be prepared before we went down to the river. He held it close and chanted softly for a while, then he placed it on my head. It sat there soft and docile, little claws tucked in and feathers soft against my skin. He murmured and waved incense in front of the chicken's face and I felt its body get heavy and droop. It had gone into trance. The Brahmin lifted it and said, "Let's go," and we headed down the dark streets together, up the hill, past Tiger Bazaar, past all the houses and the mission hospital, across the deserted field above the river. We could hear the water rushing and see flecks of foam in the moonlight. The Brahmin's friend had a flashlight and illuminated the embankment so we could make our way down. I felt nervous and tired.

"I am going to call the spirits," the Brahmin said. "They will come to my body and speak with you."

"Great," I thought, "a conversation with demons at the graveyard. What am I doing here?" The Brahmin's friend held the chicken, still drooping. The Brahmin began to chant, soft sounds, then staccato, then soft again, then harsh, guttural sounds. He started shaking. Then he roared at me and started talking about my illness. He asked me by whom I had been treated.

"A shaman in Tebas village," I replied, "and the doctor."

"You lie!" he shouted. "There is another."

"No," I replied. "No one beyond this Brahmin here."

"You lie!" he said again. "What about the lama?" I remembered that Prema lama had checked my pulse and said something like, "Mm. A possible possession."

"Yes," I said, "I met with a lama."

"Mmm," he said, sounding satisfied. He muttered and shook for a while. "A witch has set some powerful spirits on you," he said. "She comes to your room from the north."

"But there are no houses to the north of my room," I said.

"Fool!" he shouted. "There is a path outside your window to the north. She comes and speaks to you there." The path was there. People did stop and speak to me at the window. No one there had ever been to the village that I lived in. The Brahmin shook some more. He muttered and shouted. Then the sounds got lower, the shaking softer. He lay down on the sand.

His friend lit some incense and waved it under his nose. His breathing became more restful. He opened his eyes and sat up, looking around.

"A success, I think," he said, sounding like his usual self. "What did he say?" His friend told him. "Now the chicken," he said, "and I will make your amulet. We must give him the chicken." He took out a square piece of paper with drawings and mantras on it. Then he held the chicken and slit its throat. Wings flapped. I looked away. He squirted some blood on the paper. His friend wrapped up the chicken's body. He held the paper and murmured over it, folding it into smaller and smaller squares and finally wrapping it with red thread. Then he tied it around my neck. "This will protect you," he said.

We walked back up to the street together, then parted, home being in different directions. Tom accompanied me back to my Thakali friends' place.

"Pretty strange, huh?" he said. "Do you feel better?"

"About the same, so far," I said. "Tired. Thanks for coming." I went in and slept a dull and heavy sleep with troubled dreams.

Sometimes I thought I felt a little better after the exorcism, but nothing dramatic. I felt uneasy wearing an amulet soaked with the blood of a sacrificed animal. Later, when I had to go to Kathmandu, I dropped it into the sacred waters of the river that runs below the great Siva temple. "Mother Ganges cleanses all," said my friend Noel as it sank under the murky waters. "I don't really like," I had said to him, "having a pact with a demon."

In the village after that, when people stopped to talk with me outside my window in Tebas, I wondered: "Whom have I offended? Who would wish me ill?" I asked Ama about possible witches. It was the dry season and people spread grain on mats outside to prepare it for storage. Women sat in the courtyards weaving with their looms and chatted. Funerals took place here and there and I attended them. Maila lama came down from the north with his assistants to purify households by chanting the sacred texts. I went to Cliff Shelter and spent the day in an attic room pouring tea for the lamas and listening as they drummed and chanted and played the long-horns. I felt peaceful in the shadowy room as people came and went all day, paying respects, chatting. I went to see Pajon. There were days where I had to stay in bed, but most of the time I could manage.

I came back the long way from Pajon's house, down the mountain via Cliff Shelter, so I could check my mail. I arrived in the evening and had dinner with Bhimsen's family. There was going to be a ritual in Tebas that I wanted to attend the next day. A little worn from walking, I went to bed early. They put me in an alcove in the back of the family quarters. I stirred when they came in later and climbed into their beds by the light of a small lamp, but drifted back to sleep more comfortable for their being there.

In the morning, I woke in the dim light with pain deep in my stomach. I felt faint. Bhimsen came in and said, "Child, if you want to see the ritual in Tebas, you'll need to be leaving soon." I told him I was not very well but would be up in a little while. I lay there under the warm blankets and stared at the beams across the ceiling. The pain thudded inside me. "Try," I thought. "I've just got to try." I had been ill for several months by then and knew about trying. It was the local response to illness. When I had been ill in the village once long before, little Seyli had come into my room. "Please get up, sister," she said. "People who stay in bed die. If you get up you will feel better." My thoughts echoed her comment. "If I get up, I will feel better," I thought. I decided to walk down to the river and splash my face. I was a little wobbly but I could stand. I stepped slowly to the door and held on for a moment. I was all right. I walked across the stone street and circled round behind the temple. The morning was gray but bright. I stepped across the rocks and headed for the water. The Gurung woman who lived next door to Bhimsen was washing her clothes a bit further down.

After two or three steps, I felt faint. The pain amplified. That's all I remember, though I must have fallen, probably face up since I felt the sensation of light all around me. The next thing I knew, Bhimsen was calling, "Child, child," and he lifted me up and carried me to their living quarters, laying me out on their large bed. He covered me with a blanket. I couldn't talk. The pain pulsed through my stomach and my sense of the surroundings faded in and out. The room started to fill up with people, staring at me curiously, some I knew, some I didn't. I remembered Mina's death, everyone gathered there, watching. I found my voice. "Please send them out, Father," I said. He cleared the room.

"We could rub your legs," he said, "massage them with oil." I had done that for Mina. She had died within the hour.

"No," I said, "please no." I faded out again, riding the waves of pain. Each time my attention returned, he was there pacing back and forth like he did in the street, hands behind his back. I thought of people who would miss me when I died. I could not think of much because the pain was so absorbing. I felt sad. Amid the waves, there was a great stabbing feeling, then something shifted. The pain began to ebb: little pulses, softening. Gentler rolls of sensation. The room came into focus. I felt the pillow under me and the soft quilt across my skin. I watched Bhimsen cross the room and return. His eyes rested on me. "A little better?" he asked.

"A little better," I replied. He paced some more, then called out the door. He approached my bed with a glass.

"A little milk?" he asked. I nodded. He lifted me off the pillow and cradled my shoulders, tipping the glass against my lips. I drank the sweet, cool liquid, just a sip or two, then he set me gently back. After a while he went out. It was late afternoon by then. The Gurung neighbor came in. She sat by the bed in a chair, and held my hand. I rested.

The light outside poured across the pavement. There was a plant near one window with red flowers. The leaves looked green and succulent, rich in their fullness, and the flowers seemed languid, almost luminous. I knew that it was time for me to go.

I felt I had in some way died and been reborn that day, lost the world framed in that window, then been restored to it. Now I was free to go. I belonged there. It would always be part of me. I felt if I wanted to live I had to go on. The incident reminded me that people die from illness and that life could be burningly beautiful, not to be given up lightly or soon.

When I came home I told Ama. I said I would leave right away. I could not bear to do it slowly.

"Yes," she said. "You have been different these last months. Like your heart-mind was contracted. Not so easy as before."

"I have been ill," I said.

"I don't think it was the illness that made you difficult," she said. "Illness alone does not do that." I felt sad, chastened. After dinner she followed me out to my room. We sat on my bed.

"Your country is different," she said.

"Yes," I replied.

"I have had so many children," she said, "one after another without rest. The other night I had a dream that there was another child in my womb.

It was a little boy, and its penis protruded through my navel. I woke up distressed. It wears you down, so many children. Some die. It is so hard. If it is not necessary to your honor in your country, do not have children. You will find life easier. Or maybe have just one."

"Children are not necessary to honor in America," I said.

"And you must write to us," she said. "I do not write, but my son will answer your letters. I will tell you how to write a proper letter. You have to give respectful greetings, then blessings to the little ones. Say that by the grace of the gods you are well and that you pray that the gods should keep us well, too. Say that you pray each day that we will meet again soon. Then give whatever news. Then say that's all for now and sign it your loving daughter. You can't just write any old thing that comes to mind. It looks nice if you write a proper letter."

"I will write," I said. "And I will come back. As soon as I am able. I have my schooling to do. But I will come back in three years like the soldiers do, like your sons in the army."

"Our daughter, too, will come back in three years. That's good," she said.

I left via Torr, to say good-bye to Pajon. We did not let other people know I was going. Ama wanted to keep it quiet. She did not want to say good-bye to me in a crowd, with all the wishes and banter and people watching. "Everyone would come," she said. I did not want that either. I left Apa and the others in the house. He blessed me. The children wished me well. Ama and Tson walked around with me across the top of the village and past the water tap. It was breakfast time and most people were inside. We continued down the path to the waterfall where the trail curves round to the other side of the mountain. "We'll stop here," Ama said. Tson stood next to her. I hugged Tson. She looked surprised. I covered my hair with my shawl and bowed down to Ama's feet. I rose and looked at her, speechless, and tears poured down my face. Drops trickled down her cheeks.

"Go well, Ernestine," she said.

"Stay well, Ama," I replied. I pressed my palms together and turned away. When I got to the bend that would take me out of sight, I turned back. Ama and Tson were still standing there next to the ferns while the water rushed down. We looked at each other for a few moments, then I walked on.

8.
Return

This is the last memory I have of her, my sometime mother: the ferns behind her, the sheltering cliff, her eyes sad but steady, Tson tall beside her. I came back in three years as promised to find the world split open and bleeding. Ama had died. There had been a gap of a few weeks in letters, but no one had mentioned that she was ill. She had died of cancer two months before I arrived. Tson was in India with her husband when I got to the village. Apa was at home with the smaller children. Agai came to visit. Bunti, the adopted servant girl, came to see me from her married home. Ama had arranged her marriage to a soldier in a nearby village.

"She saw that I made a decent marriage," Bunti said. "She was good to me. I came as often as I could to help during her illness."

Apa said she had been sick for some time. Agai's husband had taken her to Kathmandu for medical treatment. She had surgery but the cancer was too advanced to be cured. She was better for a while, but then relapsed. Apa told me how the stewardess had helped her down the steps of the plane on her return and given her some flowers. She had been all right for a bit, able to walk and eat, gaining strength. Her family was delighted. She was optimistic. Then the cancer returned and desolated her in every way.

Ama did not want to die. "When will I see my son in the army?" she had said. "When will I see my American daughter? And my little ones? It is a sin to leave small children. I will not be a person any more. I will not be a person." She cried and said these things and could not be consoled, Bunti told me. I held back tears as she spoke but little hiccupping sobs escaped, and finally I wept with abandon. Bunti held me and cried, too, then stroked my hair and said, "Enough, enough," while she dried her own tears. I was moved to know that Ama might have thought of me. I sat by the hearth looking at the soft brown of the clay floor and walls, and I missed her. The house seemed empty. "Her son in the army sent a sweater," said Bunti, "and it got here the day she died. A dark blue one. We put it on her effigy at the funeral."

People said her brother, Neem Bahadur, was distraught with grief when Ama died. When he spoke of her to me, on the veranda of his house in Pokhara one evening, there were tears in his eyes. "Her death was a great sorrow to me," he said.

I went to see Pajon and sat with her at the inn in Torr. She was sad and remorseful because her arthritis had prevented her walking to see Ama during her illness. She had heard people talking of her death as she woke from a nap. "I was having a dream of looking for her, looking for her in a yogurt pot, then I woke and heard them talking of a death. 'Who is it?' I asked. 'Who has died?' I knew, though, it was her. From childhood we had been so close." She wept. Pajon's son helped carry the bier to the crema- tion ground. "It was so light," he said, "you would hardly know anything was on it."

Everywhere I went people made me cry. They would speak of Ama and watch my face. "I remember when you came here and she had put her gold jewelry on you. All up your arm, the beautiful bracelets. You sat just here and had tea together." I would burst into tears and they would wait, then pat my back perhaps, and say, "Enough, enough." Some people cried at the sight of me. "You were always together. I miss her so much when I see you." Others provoked my tears, then joined me and we wept together. The monsoon rains poured down and I went from place to place and cried. She was not there but her world received me. It gave me a place for my grief. It let me know I was home.

I go back when I can. I have become close to my sisters. Agai lives in a tall house at Tiger Bazaar in Pokhara and Maili is just a short distance away in a neighborhood filled with families from Tebas, a street of white- washed bungalows with pleasant porches. Except for one brief meeting, I have not seen Tson in all my visits. She has four sons who must be nearly grown and has spent many years in India by now. I have never met her husband, Ama's eldest son. Maila and Saila, teenaged boys on my first trip, have also married and are in the British army, abroad more often than at home. Seyli, whom Ama thought looked like me, still has her strong good spirit and Kanchi, four when I first met her, has grown into a shapely woman. They are both married now, too.

Apa remarried after a time, taking Mina's elder sister, Rita, as a wife. He took some criticism, too, because of her youth, but they seem well suited to each other. He cites the great god Siva as his model, who married the beautiful Parvati after his first wife died. Now he has another son.

Pajon remained in Torr with her son Siva and his wife and two daughters. I saw a picture of Siva's wife in *National Geographic* several months ago, in an article on conservation in the Annapurna region. She was cooking on a fuel-efficient stove and smiling up at the camera. I hope Pajon's grandchildren "make life bright," as she said. Her arthritis has worsened and she stays mainly at home.

When I last went to Nepal, in 1987, I stayed with Maili in Pokhara. The monsoon was in full force and the paths to the mountains were treacherous, the winter bridges washed out. Pajon heard I was there and sent a messenger with a Polaroid photo of herself sitting on the veranda of the inn wrapped in a white shawl, direct brown eyes looking out. "She asked me to tell you, 'Come, no matter what,'" the messenger said. I looked out at the mountains overhung with mists and thought of the paths I knew so well, but pregnant and exhausted, I feared the trip. I sent her the present I had brought for her and a note filled with love and regret. I hope I will have another chance to come, no matter what. Then I can bring my daughter and we can all sleep around the hearth, lying in the dark and talking as the fire dies down. In the meantime, I keep her photo in my study. It sits above me as I write, next to a poem by a friend, across from the window where I look out on birch trees.

I did not get to see Bhimsen either on my last trip. I often wonder how he is. I recently met a Sherpa man in the Adirondacks, a guide who frequently travels through the region I lived in. He told me he thinks Bhimsen is still in Cliff Shelter housing travelers at his inn. I hope so. Before I left, there was a grand wedding when he brought a bride for his eldest son. Since his daughter Manju asked to remain at home until the last possible moment, her parents married her in her early twenties to a man whose family runs an inn at Horse Water. I heard she is happy there.

Dharmamitra's nephew has become a monk. His religious commitment explains why he had never married and was so often with his aunt. On my last visit he seemed likely to take over the Pokhara vihar.

And where am I? Rochester, New York, where I started this story, in a house on a quiet street with stands of birches in the back. A crow caws outside. Around me is the lush green of late summer. I live with my daughter and her beloved pets: the sparrow she rescued as a chick two summers ago, the chinchilla (very soft, not much personality), and her charming and insouciant dog. I teach at a university in a well-known school of music, though I am not at all musical, in their humanities department, which is like a tiny liberal arts college within their musical realm. When my daughter was smaller she called it my Beautiful Workplace because of the red carpets and chandeliers that run along the way to my office in the back of the theater. My students are passionate and devoted to their music. What they seem to like best of what I offer them are the stories of Nepal. They are hungry to have ideas filled out with real people. The first year I taught here I assigned a book by a friend that we all enjoyed very much. "Where is your book?" asked a girl. "We want to read it." Here it is.

Ama is gone. The world I lived in is shattered, though the basic qualities of it are still intact, I think: a sense of honor, a value on graciousness, a belief in the need for endurance, because life is marked by suffering. The old world no longer has a location: there, bounded, the village as "our own country," marked by these rivers and this mountainside. Fragments of it fly out or wither: aristocratic families leaving, ceremonies canceled because the mayor thinks them useless or backward. It is not as it once seemed, complete and sufficient in itself. But the great slopes are still there, carved with terraces and the river tumbles and gushes, singing over rocks in the winter, swelling and thundering down the gorge in the summer. Eagles fly below the village, then wheel and loop up, higher, until you can see the sun coming through their feathers.

Many fine people have stayed in the village, and new ideas have come: techniques of conservation, the thought that girls might not marry so young, vaccinations for the children. It is an effervescent time, though I miss the harmony of the old days with the land marked by its sacred spots, the year by its stately ceremonial progression, all of it revolving around our courtyard (headman's house as hub of the universe), the uncanny surrounding us, forest filled with magic dangers. I forget the fear of witchcraft and the cost of order. There are new fears and new costly orders, though, lacking the elegance and richness of the old ones.

Some of what I love of that world has come west. There are Buddhist and Hindu temples in Rochester, and a store where I can buy the same spices we used in the village and rent the same Hindi movies that Maili and Agai have seen in Pokhara. There is a blond physician who practices traditional Indian medicine with considerable skill and effectiveness. I speak Nepali with friends on the phone. I find these fragments in unexpected places, easing the disjunction of my life. I sometimes dream I am wandering through the bazaar, looking for something, but no one can show me where to find it.

Perhaps it is courage and imagination. That is what propelled me there so young and what allowed Ama to make me so suddenly an intimate. "I'll be your mother": what a burden of responsibility; what a risk. What a gift it was to me, who came to her so filled with pain and hope. What she left me with was more pain and hope; the pain of knowing and loving, the hope of knowing and loving, the inevitable reality of loss.

Conceptual Context
and Related Readings

Social Life

The Gurungs have lived for centuries in a world rich with interconnections, a sophisticated universe. Their views of life have been influenced by the elaborate intellectual traditions of Buddhism, and to some degree by Hinduism, too. Their locality has included a number of diverse peoples with ways of life that differed in large and small ways from their own. Nearby were villages of high-caste Hindus following Brahmanic rules of conduct; Magars, whose life styles were similar in many respects, especially in their egalitarian ethos, to those of Gurungs; and Thakalis, another Buddhist people more closely aligned with monastic interpretations of religion, and more involved in trade than farming.

For those who want to learn more about the Gurungs, good general ethnographies of Gurung life include *The Gurungs of Nepal: Conflict and Change in a Village Society*, by Donald Messerschmidt (Warminster, U.K.: Aris and Phillips, 1976), and the succinct *Gurungs of Nepal: A Guide to the Gurungs*, by Alan Macfarlane and Ganesh Man Gurung (Kathmandu: Ratna Pustak Bhandar, 1990), as well as the classic and comprehensive *Les Gurungs: Une population himalayenne du Népal*, by Bernard Pignède (The Hague: Mouton, 1966). *Resources and Population: A Study of the Gurungs of Nepal*, by Alan Macfarlane (Cambridge: Cambridge University Press, 1976) addresses issues of subsistence and ecology, as does *Form and Function: A Study of Nutrition, Adaptation, and Social Inequality in Three Gurung Villages of the Nepal Himalayas*, by Simon Strickland (London: Smith-Gordon, 1997). Pirkko Moisala discusses the important place of music in Gurung society, in *Music and Cultural Cognition: Continuity and Change in the Gurung Music of Nepal* (Jyvaskyla: Gummerus Kirjapaino Oy, 1991). For an engaging account of a journey in a direction opposite to my own, in which an elderly Gurung woman tours the United States with her adopted American son, see *Aama in America: A Journey of the Heart* by Broughton Coburn (New York: Anchor Books, 1995).

Although Gurungs had been going abroad as Gurkha soldiers in the British and Indian armies for generations, their social world was defined primarily in local terms during the period that I lived with them. In the technical terminology of anthropology, the structure of Gurung society at the time I lived in Nepal would be described as *patrilineal* (with property passed from father to sons, and lineage and clan defined through the father), with a *cross-cousin marriage system* (so that brides were brought into the household from the lineage or clan of the groom's mother's brother or his father's sister). Cross-cousin marriage perpetuates the links between lineages and clans, because it repeats intermarriages generation after generation. Marriage was *patrilocal*, which meant that the bride came to live in her husband's household, and *village exogamy* was preferred, which meant that people thought it best if the bride and groom came from different villages, as this would help establish a wider range of relationships. This creates a system in which the woman, acting as the link between clans in Gurung society, must suffer personal displacement in knitting the larger social group together. After she settles into her new home, though, it gives a woman the vantage point of two households, a broad social perspective, and a large network of intimates. Rules of descent and marriage, which can be abstracted and mapped almost like mathematical equations, have a strong impact on people's experiences and emotional lives.

The lives of Himalayan women are described in rich detail in *The Words and Worlds of Tamang Women from Highland Nepal*, by Kathryn March (Ithaca, N.Y.: Cornell University Press, 2001), with issues of caste highlighted in *Dangerous Wives and Sacred Sisters: The Social and Symbolic Roles of High-Caste Women in Nepal*, by Lynn Bennett (New York: Columbia University Press, 1983), and *On the Edge of the Auspicious: Gender and Caste in Nepal*, by Mary Cameron (Champaign: University of Illinois Press, 1998). *Spirited Women: Gender, Religion, and Cultural Identity in the Nepal Hima-*

laya, by Joanne Watkins (New York: Columbia University Press, 1996), addresses the impact of the global economy on women's experience and spheres of influence, and *In the Circle of the Dance: Notes of an Outsider in Nepal*, by Katherine Guneratne (Ithaca, N.Y.: Cornell University Press, 1999), explores, from a personal point of view, the confrontation of women in a lowland village with foreign perspectives and ways of life. I wrote about the life cycle of Gurung women in an early article called "The Women of Tebas: Feminine Perspectives in Gurung Culture," *Kailash: A Journal of Himalayan Studies* 8, nos.1–2(1981):45–69.

Moral and Religious Concepts

Other ethnic groups in Nepal share some of the concerns about human relationship and concepts of the self described in this book. The universe of human interactions and moral understandings among the Newars of the Kathmandu valley is described elegantly in *Moral Knowing in a Sacred Hindu City*, by Steven Parish (New York: Columbia University Press, 1994). The implications of such understandings for social practice are examined in his *Hierarchy and Its Discontents: Culture and the Politics of Consciousness in Caste Society* (Philadelphia: University of Pennsylvania Press, 1996), and in *Contested Hierarchies: A Collaborative Ethnography of Caste Among the Newars of Kathmandu*, edited by David Gellner and Declan Quigley (Oxford: Oxford University Press, 1999).

In *Body and Soul: The Aesthetics of Illness and Healing in the Nepal Himalayas* (Philadelphia: University of Pennsylvania Press, 1992), Robert Desjarlais provides a graceful account of the relation of ideas of illness and healing to concepts of the heart-mind among the Yolmo of Helambu. Robert Paul addresses some parallel concepts in *The Tibetan Symbolic World: Psychoanalytic Explorations* (Chicago: University of Chicago Press, 1982). The concept of the heart-mind exists in many parts of South Asia and provides a way of conceiving feelings in terms that integrate emotion with body, mind, and social life. I have written about this in detail in an article called "Concepts of the Person among the Gurungs of Nepal," *American Ethnologist* 16, no.1(1989):75–86.

Buddhism has many variants and intertwines with many beliefs in the

Himalayan region. The Gurungs participate in the Nyingma school of Buddhism, and their practice has historically been non-monastic, inter-mingled with everyday life, in some ways reflecting shamanic orienta-tions. Many divine beings are considered present in their world, and they did not when I lived there compartmentalize these as Buddhist, Hindu, or shamanistic, though they recognized the distinctness of these histori-cal traditions and would call on the different religious practitioners asso-ciated with them for different tasks.

The Buddhist mortuary ritual, or *pae*, plays out ideas about self, re-lationship, and the cosmos that have been deeply important in Gurung understandings of life. To learn more about the Buddhist context out of which many Gurung beliefs grow, read Geoffrey Samuel, *Civilized Sha-mans: Buddhism in Tibetan Societies* (Washington, D.C.: Smithsonian Insti-tution Press, 1993). For an interesting comparison, see David Holmberg's exposition of the Tamang religious system in *Order in Paradox: Myth, Ritual, and Exchange among Nepal's Tamang* (Ithaca, N.Y.: Cornell Uni-versity Press, 1989). In *Himalayan Dialogue: Tibetan Lamas and Gurung Shamans in Nepal* (Madison: University of Wisconsin Press, 1989), Stan Mumford juxtaposes some Gurung religious practices with those of a nearby Tibetan community, and illuminates their parallels and contrasts.

Sherry Ortner writes about the Sherpas' relation to Buddhism in two books: *Sherpas Through their Rituals* (Cambridge: Cambridge University Press, 1978) and *High Religion: A Cultural and Political History of Sherpa Buddhism* (Princeton, N.J.: Princeton University Press, 1989). These de-scribe some complexities of the relationship between community and reli-gious life, as do several books focusing on the Newars, including *Meso-cosm: Hinduism and the Organization of a Traditional Newar City in Nepal*, by Robert Levy with Kedar Rajopdhyaya (Berkeley: University of Califor-nia Press, 1990); *Monk, Householder, and Tantric Priest: Newar Buddhism and Its Hierarchy of Ritual*, by David Gellner (Cambridge: Cambridge Uni-versity Press, 1992); and *Mahayana Buddhist Texts from Nepal: Narratives and Rituals of Newar Buddhism*, by Todd Lewis (Albany: State University of New York Press, 2000). For a rich account of spirit possession and sha-manic practices in Nepal, see *The Rulings of the Night: An Ethnography of Nepalese Shaman Oral Texts*, by Gregory Maskarinec (Madison: University of Wisconsin Press, 1995).

Change and Contemporary Views

Global forces have become more influential over time in Gurung life and elsewhere in Nepal. Several scholars have addressed the implications of this in a volume entitled *Selves in Time and Place: Identities, Experience, and History in Nepal*, edited by Debra Skinner, Alfred Pach, and Dorothy Holland (Boulder, Colo.: Rowman and Littlefield, 1998). Various authors have addressed different dimensions of these changes in their own books as well. *Fashioning Modernity in Kathmandu*, by Mark Liechty (Princeton, N.J.: Princeton University Press, forthcoming), offers an elegant perspective on the meanings of consumerism in the lives of city dwellers in the Kathmandu valley, and Laura Ahearn gives an illuminating account of the ways in which concepts of love and their enactments in relationship are being reshaped, in *Invitations to Love: Literacy, Love Letters, and Social Change in Nepal* (Ann Arbor: University of Michigan Press, 2001).

The Sherpas have been the objects of global scrutiny for decades. James Fisher describes the impact of development on Sherpa social and economic life in *Sherpas: Reflections on Change in Himalayan Nepal* (Berkeley: University of California Press, 1990). Vincanne Adams shows how images of Sherpas have been transformed in a global context in *Tigers of the Snows and Other Virtual Sherpas: An Ethnography of Himalayan Encounters* (Princeton, N.J.: Princeton University Press, 1996), and Sherry Ortner reveals ways in which mountaineering has affected Sherpas in *Life and Death on Mt. Everest: Sherpas and Himalayan Mountaineering* (Princeton, N.J.: Princeton University Press, 1999).

In the past few decades, the social and political situation has altered profoundly in Nepal, the climactic event being the revolution of 1990. Aspirations for change and the influence of political events have been discussed in Dor Bahadur Bista's *Fatalism and Development: Nepal's Struggle for Modernization* (Calcutta: Orient Longman, 1991), an analysis of social and cultural obstacles to improved economic conditions; and in a thoughtful collection of essays, some responding to Bista's book, called *Nepal in the Nineties*, ed. Michael Hutt (Delhi: Oxford University Press, 1994). Vincanne Adams addresses the intersection of politics and health, in *Doctors for Democracy: Health Care Professionals in the Nepal Revolution* (Cambridge: Cambridge University Press, 1998), as does Judith Justice in reference to another political arena, in *Policies, Plans and People: Foreign Aid and Health Development in Nepal* (Berkeley: University of California Press, 1986). The interdisciplinary journal *Studies in Nepali History and Society* (Kathmandu: Mandala Book Point) provides a forum in which many contemporary issues and their historical foundations are discussed. I have written about urbanization and changing concepts of honor in an article entitled "Situating Persons: Constructions of Honor in Gurung Society," published in the volume edited by Skinner, Pach, and Holland, noted above.

My responses to life, intellectual and otherwise, have been strongly conditioned by the perspectives of the people with whom I lived in Nepal. Perhaps I felt compelled to write this book in personal terms (it was not a considered decision) in order to give their worldview precedence, rather than subsuming it in someone else's theoretical perspective. It is, of course, filtered through me, but not in service here of an intellectual agenda. Implicit though, I suppose, is a desire to heed Ashis Nandy's call, in *The Intimate Enemy: Loss and Recovery of Self Under Colonialism* (Delhi: Oxford University Press, 1983), to take seriously non-Western theories of existence and representations of reality. Some of these are self-consciously local, with no assertion of relevance beyond an immediate context, though I have found that, even so, they may illumine aspects of experience far beyond that. Others, like Buddhism, claim universal significance and speak to other articulations of life, including the intellectual traditions of the West, in varieties of ways that are well worth exploring. A book that links these realms with special grace and insight, in a way particularly relevant to my work here, is *Meeting the Great Bliss Queen: Buddhists, Feminists, and the Art of the Self*, by Anne Carolyn Klein (Boston: Beacon Press, 1995). As such dialogues develop, and as they are pursued in the classroom and in public space, I hope they might contribute to a world in which many have the privilege of having their deepest experience informed by multiple points of view.

Index

Acknowledgments

One person who was essential to the launching of this project and nurtured it gently along the way, replied when I thanked him, "You wrote it yourself." This is true, but the affection and interest of my friends sustained me. Prominent among these were Peggy Rosenthal and George Dardess who read the manuscript-in-progress and encouraged me, in the broadest sense of the word, as well as providing good counsel. My daughter Ursula's loving presence makes my life radiant and reminds me in all my work of what is most important. Colleagues in the Humanities Department at the Eastman School of Music and the University of Rochester's Department of Anthropology have provided indispensable warmth, hospitality, and intellectual companionship, as have Huma Ahmed-Ghosh, Mark Busse, Brinda Dalal, Mary Des Chene, Robert Desjarlais, Sara Dickey, Nancy Foster, Karma Kumari Gurung, David Holmberg, Philip Kapleau, Victoria Kieburtz, Bodhin Kjolhede, Ellen Koskoff, Lauren Leve, Kathryn March, Gregory Maskarinec, Sheila McCabe, Steven Parish, Naomi Quinn, Maimoona Ramaswamy, Geoffrey Samuel, Rita Shakya, Yohko Tsuji, and Richard von Sturmer.

The families of Jagat Bahadur Gurung and Til Kumari Gurung have shown unfailing graciousness and kind interest in my work over the years, as have Gananath and Ranjini Obeyesekere and Sherry Ortner. More people than I can name provided a critically important "good climate" in which to work. Friends, colleagues, and strangers provided help in the final stages of this project. Franlee Frank expressed welcoming enthusiasm for the newly finished manuscript and offered valuable advice on finding a home for it, as did Ayala Emmett and Naomi Quinn. Tracy Burdick and Naomi Pless helped to select the photographs. Kirin Narayan provided indispensable wisdom and guidance throughout the process of bringing this book to publication. My work is stronger for her comments and those of another, anonymous, reviewer. I thank Paul Stoller for his helpful remarks and suggestions, and deeply appreciate his sending the book to Patricia Smith at the University of Pennsylvania Press, whose sensitivity, humor, and insight has made every aspect of the editorial process a pleasure.

Special gratitude to Amala Wrightson, who went over the first draft of the manuscript with meticulous and loving care, focusing and refining the prose. For the Gurung people, whom I so deeply respect and admire, my thanks are beyond words.

what is home?

underlying themes of conflict -
wanting to belong / going home
Chptr. 3 ℃4 about Nepali life
rest - about herself
personal exp. in moment
  ↳ later - mature reflections